THE
MANY
GRAPE

1st Edition

Joseph Picard

For information, feedback or other questions, contact the author.

Joseph Picard joe@ozero.ca

Cover art by Joseph Picard
Other books by Joseph can be found at www.ozero.ca

Editorial consult for The One Grapes:
Alan Seeger of Five59 Publishing
http://five59.com/

/// WARNING! \\\

Aside from my usual "UK English" warning, there is also terrible art.

The quality of the art is independent of me using the letter U more than the Americans. The art is terrible because... well, at this point, I may as well leave it to the foreword to explain.

Either way, it's still 'colour', not 'color'.

And ZED, not "ZEE".

FOREWORD

(Quick note: to skip past the content from "The One Grapes", go to page 51)

Well, the forward is updated...
So, here's where I explain myself... again.

Long long ago, in the latter third of the second year of the new century, my epic battle of man-on-mountain-bike against the front end of a Ford Mustang ended as quickly as it had started. So, it was... pretty instantaneous and one-sided. Worst epic ever. Really, it flies In the face of what epic means, doesn't it? Even if you filmed it in slow motion, it would scarcely fill a half minute.

Unless you count the wait for the ambulance. Oh, and the resulting lifelong paraplegia. That ends up a bit longer. No violent chariot races races for Liz Taylor, though, Not *yet*. I'm not writing this posthumously so that could still happen.

Note to self- if I ever do another book in the Lifehack universe, have a gladiator-style chariot race of all zombies, performed for a zombie Liz.

ANYWAY.... 14 years later, I suffered my first "pressure wound", a common hazard for paraplegics. It resulted in a nearly two month stay in the hospital. (Shorter than the six months back in 2001, after the epic battle, but two months is two months, and this was done without such joys as morphine, which tend to make hospital-time even fuzzier than it already is.)

During this time, I became re-familiarized with hospital food. It was better than expectations, but my expectations were not high at all. Yes, it's on the bland side; for medical reasons, the kitchen doesn't dish out salt and spice. They do what they can. I guess.

The meals come to one's room on a tray, with a paper slip. The paper slip has a small satisfaction survey on one side, and an inventory of what's on the tray on the other. I filled out a survey when I first noticed it, and didn't feel the need to fill out another.

Then, I saw "HALF BANANA" on one of the sheets. So be fair, it was kind of a huge half banana, but the term immediately made me think of Robocop, so...

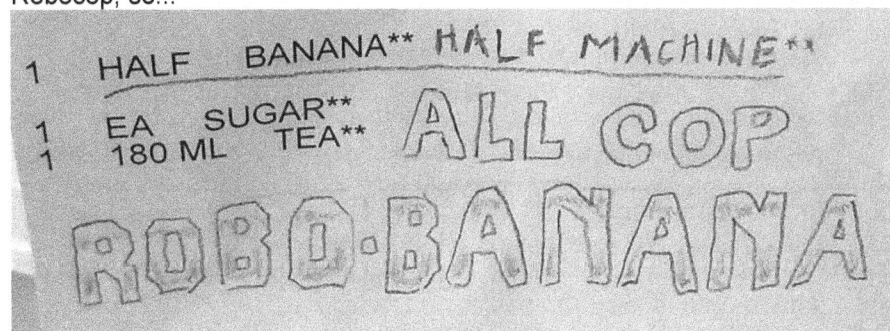

3

Linda, who was the kitchen staffer who took away most of my trays, thought it was amusing enough that I was motivated to do more. This was the smallest one I did as well. If I were to re-do it, I'd draw a character to go with it.

And shortly after my escape, "The One Grapes" was born.

And then, nearly two years passed...

When I went home, the 17.5 cm deep wound was not healed. It was down to about 10 or 9 cm. But the massive infection that had gotten into me along with the wound had been defeated.

For two years, a nurse came to the house roughly three times a week, to monitor the wound progress, and change the dressings. I was essentially bed-ridden for a while after returning home, with my 'uptime' increasing as the wound healed...

And one day, almost two years after my first hospital stay started, a nurse re-dressing the wound says "Not lookin' that great today."

And another day, "Looks a bit rough."

"Looking kinda serious."

"I think we need to have a team meeting."

At that last one, I began making a mental note of things I wanted to pack. Another hospital stay was inevitable at that point.

Soon I was faced with the same food. The menu hadn't changed much, so ideas were further between. However, I only started doodling about half way through my first stay, and this time I was ready from the start... and a few ideas had simmered up since The One Grapes was finished.

As I write this, the end of this stay is approaching. It will have been longer than the last. (two years ago, it was seven weeks... the second stay was three months and two days.)

So, I've been doodling.

This book, The Many Grape, contains all the doodles from the One Grapes, plus everything from my second stay. Let's face it, as cute at the One Grapes was, it's pretty thin at around fifty pages.

I have somewhat revised the commentary with the old doodles, **but if you feel like skipping ahead to the all-new stuff, it starts at page 51. (look for the Taco Knight.)**

As before, on each image, you'll see I've underlined, and usually put a jagged outline around an item on the list.

That item is the one that inspired the doodle for that sheet. Some of them don't make a lot of sense if you don't know what the item inspiration is.

And some of them just don't make sense either way.
My apologies.

Also, apologies about the quality of some of the drawings.

Most of the doodles were done in a rush to get the doodle done, paper slip photographed, and back on the tray before the tray got picked up again. Imagine playing pictionary, but you have no idea how much time you actually have before you have to be done your picture.

A few non-food-slip drawings are included again. Some of *those* were done on a whim, others done for my kids- who made it a habit of requesting drawings from me of specific things, often characters from games they like. My best art is not in this book. My best art takes more time, a pen to ink them nicely, a scanner, and colouring on the computer. But those aren't as funny.

Many of the ragged-looking images suffer from papers that were creased or damaged before I got my hands on them. They were done in all pencil, then later run through software to make them as clear as possible. I considered redrawing them under more ideal conditions, but decided it would rob them of the feel of the original improvization.

Again, the kitchen staff seems to be enjoying my stupidity, so here we are again! Onward!

First, here's a doodle I also did in the hospital, with a *proper* sheet of paper, and not in a rush. And a few nice pens to ink it with. It's not great, but it's probably one of the prettiest doodles in the book.

Soak it in.

When you run into a horribly ugly, rushed picture, you can come back to this. Soothing, yes?

1   120 ML   MASHED POTATO**
1   120 ML   MIXED VEGETABLE**
1   EA   GRAPES**
1   EA   SUGAR**
1   180 ML   TEA**

"HOLD ON, HERE, I'M **ONE** GRAPES? I'M SINGULAR AND PLURAL?? LIKE A PHOTON?"

"NO, MORON, YOU'RE THINKING OF HOW PHOTONS ARE BOTH A PARTICLE AND A WAVE, NOW GO GET EATEN."

"... GET WHAT???"

LUNCH

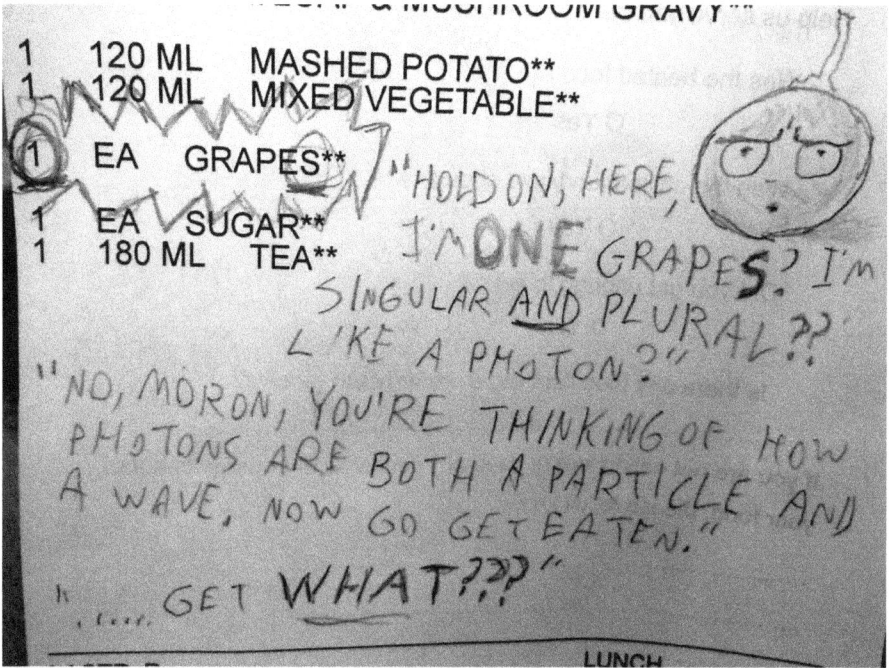

I know, I know, they mean to say something like "1 PTN (portion) GRAPES" on the list, but there it is, staring at us.

"1 EA GRAPES"

Seeing them arrive with lunch, it was quite plain... but I imagined a grape getting confused by this. An existential crisis of plurality, and the nature of his own existence.

So, 'TheOneGrape' A.K.A. TOG was born. Keep an eye out for him, you'll be seeing him again.

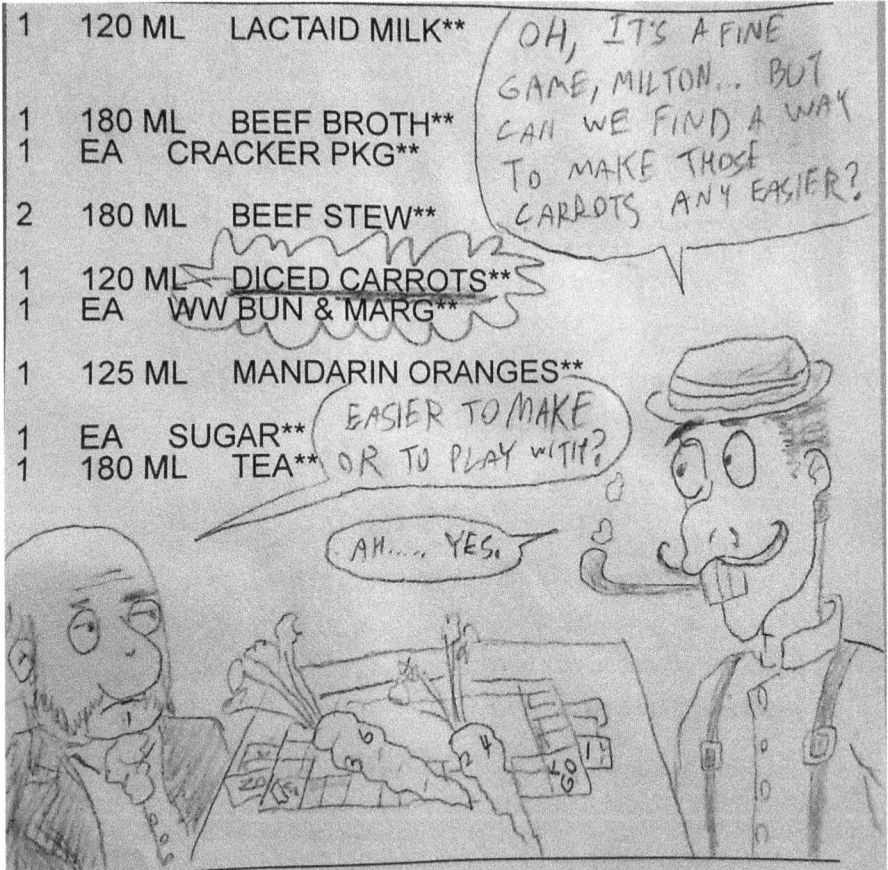

I don't have anything to say about the joke or the doodle... but can I just draw attention to another item in this meal?

BEEF BROTH. Am I supposed to dip the bun in it? I don't know, maybe I'm uncultured, but isn't a simple broth an ingredient for other things? Soup? Gravy? Hey! Beef broth was always a let-down when it showed up, when they had several nice soups that generally took that place on the tray.
No! I'm right! I just asked the internet! Broth is the *base* for making good things! I should have tried a 'stone soup' routine with it.

Those two guys in the doodle... I bet they like beef broth.

They look like the type.

2	130 GR	ROAST TURKEY & GRAVY**
1	120 ML	MASHED SWEET POTATO**
1	120 ML	PEAS & CARROTS**
1	125 ML	DICED PEACHES**
1	EA	SUGAR**
1	180 ML	TEA**
1	EA	CRANBERRY SAUCE PTN

→ SPRINKLE ON LESSER SAUCES TO CREATE CRANBERRY SAUCE.

→ DO NOT DRINK. DO NOT FEED TO TURKEYS. WE TRIED THAT ONCE. IT WAS HORRIFYING.

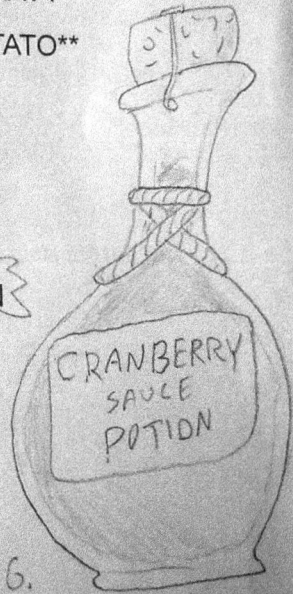

CRANBERRY SAUCE POTION

DINNER

All the oldskool gamers know what a PTN is... "POTION". The old systems weren't always capable of displaying, or sometimes even *storing* those extra letters.

Raise your hand if you remember OXYALE.

Now put your hand back down, you geeky moron, this is a book, I can't see you. R3sp3c7 for the light warriors though, brutha. Or sista.

And other folks have other notions
on other uses for cramberry potions.

EA   CRANBERRY JUICE**

EA   RANCH DRESSING**
EA   TOSSED SALAD**

120 GR   BEEF TIPS & GRAVY**

120 ML   CORN**
120 ML   MASHED POTATO**

SLICE   NANAIMO BAR**

EA   SUGAR**
180 ML   TEA**

"BEEF TIPS? YOU WANT BEEF TIPS? HERE'S ONE: CHOLESTERAL! WE'RE FULL OF IT, AND IT WILL KILL YOU! AND.... WE'RE FULL OF CYANIDE, too! And... OH. YOU MEANT COW TIPPING? well just !?#@ off, then."

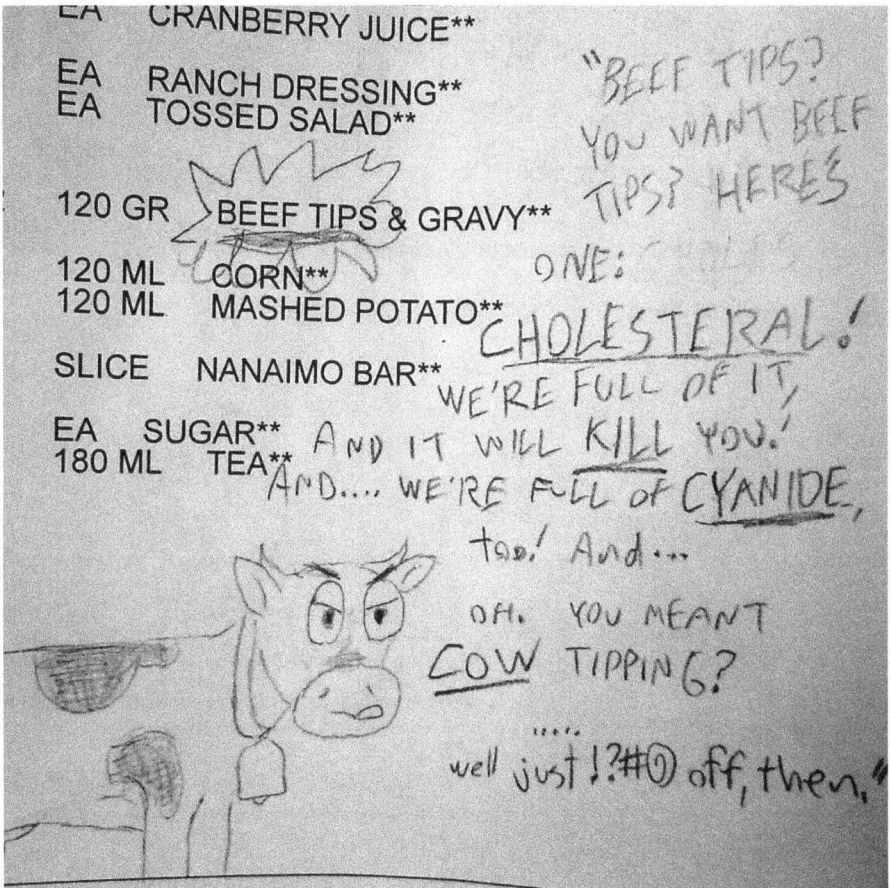

'Beef tips' was one of the best dishes I had in the hospital. I'd *heard* of the dish, but I can't say I've had it before. If I had it outside the hospital, is it much different? Better? I'll keep my eye out for it in the future...

And there's that nasty nanaimo bar... looking at me with all its lactose... Worth cheating?

Yup.

EA   GRILLED SALMON**

120 ML   DICED TURNIP**
120 ML   WHITE RICE**

125 ML   FRUIT COCKTAIL**

EA   SUGAR**
180 ML   TEA**

VERY FUNNY, GUYS: YOU KNOW WHITE RICE CAN'T JUMP.

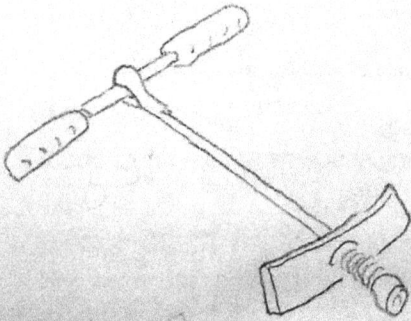

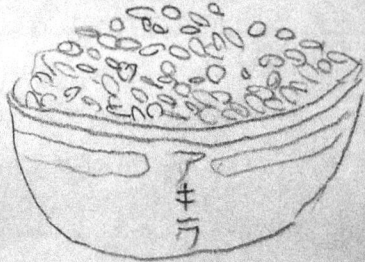

Ehh... the rice was white, but not Asian-style sticky kind of white. Not that I suppose it mattered a ton. Especially when my drawing of it looks more like rice crispies.

What does it say on the bowl?

A

KI

RA

Akira. Why? BECAUSE AKIRA, THAT'S WHY!

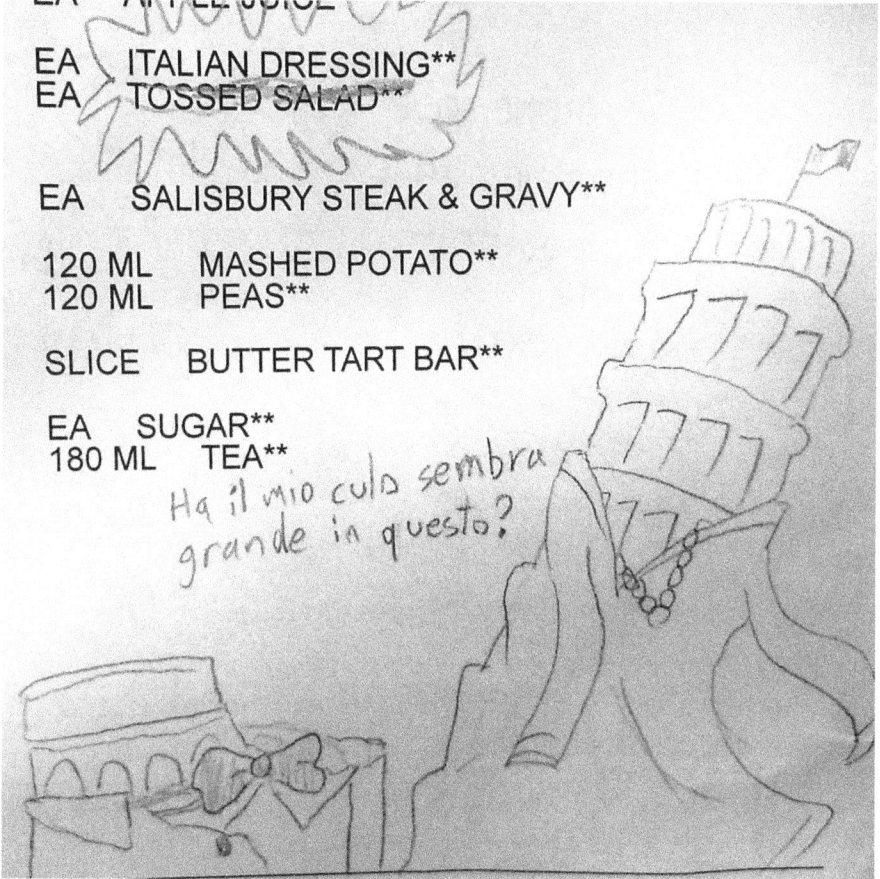

```
EA      ITALIAN DRESSING**
EA      TOSSED SALAD**

EA      SALISBURY STEAK & GRAVY**

120 ML   MASHED POTATO**
120 ML   PEAS**

SLICE    BUTTER TART BAR**

EA    SUGAR**
180 ML   TEA**
```

Ha il mio culo sembra grande in questo?

Apparently this one was a bit of a hit downstairs. That's my best rushed leaning tower of Pisa, and the Colosseum. Ya never know what will resonate with some people.

Maybe they translated the Italian line. "Does my butt look big in this?"

Shephard's pie is one of my favs, and they did a decent job with it... (sans salt...) but maybe I just appreciated it more because I'm the only one at home who likes it, so it doesn't show up at home too often.

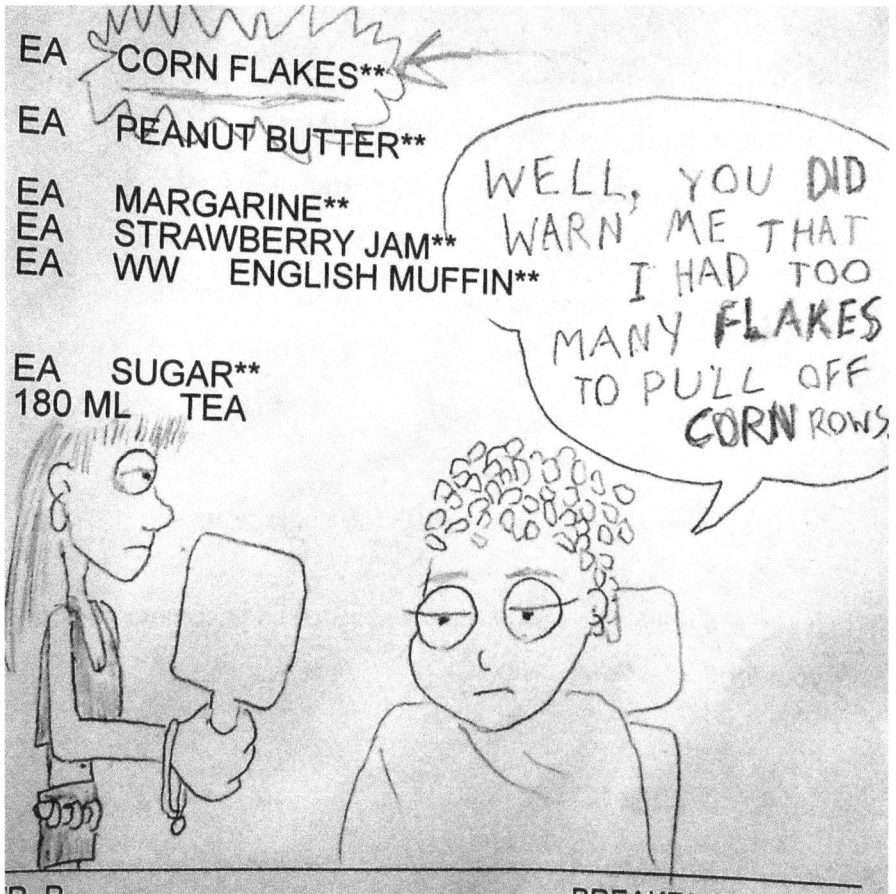

Okay, let's be honest. Her cornflake hair looks like like corn pops. Maybe I was subconsciously craving something with a bit more zip than corn flakes.

Yeah, that's right. Corn pops would have been zip. Have I complained about the lack of anything with spice on the menu? I mean, I understand why they would avoid spicy stuff, and salt... but you really have to be ready for bland.

In the arena of 'bland', they did quite well with it in general, but more than once, I'd hoped a bottle of a hot sauce would arrive from home. Or even BBQ sauce. Or vodka. Couldn't hurt.

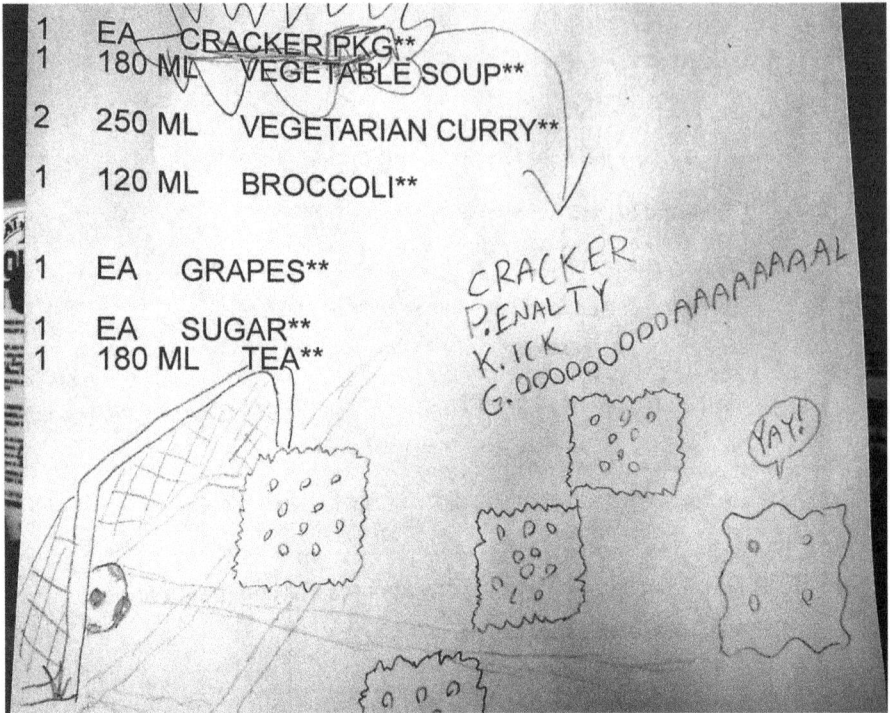

```
1   EA      CRACKER PKG**
1   180 ML  VEGETABLE SOUP**
2   250 ML  VEGETARIAN CURRY**
1   120 ML  BROCCOLI**

1   EA      GRAPES**

1   EA      SUGAR**
1   180 ML  TEA**
```

CRACKER
P.ENALTY
K.ICK
G.oooooOOOOAAAAAAAAL

YAY!

Huh. I made a sports joke.

I played in little league soccer when I was a kid. I won't say I hated it... but I just didn't get the appeal. Team sports in general turn me off. Best P.E. unit I remember in school? Cross country skiing. I don't even remember what town it was, but the school had a pile of cross country skiing gear donated to them. It's not like I was at any fancy school that would shell out for it, they...

Uh, I mean, yeah, in my high-end private school that cost a bajillion dollars a day to go to, maybe it was the school's skeet shooting team, or the polo. Or yachting.

Or skeet shooting on horseback on the yachts. It scared the horses, though, but the ones that had gone deaf were easier to handle.

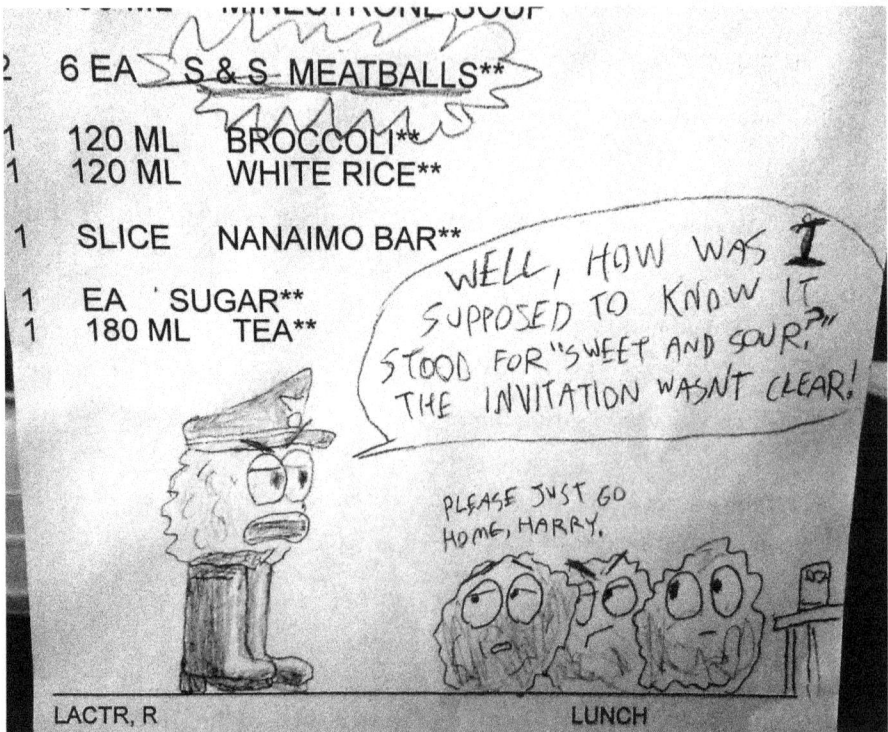

Yeah, meatballs are idiots. Yummy though.

And that friggin' nanaimo bar, with its little evil shot of lactose... The SS conspiring with lactose. I *knew* it.

(Two years later, I notice there's been nothing "sweet and sour" coming on the trays. Not the meatballs, which have a different flavour on them now, sweet and sour pork is gone, sweet and sour chicken has been replaced with CHICKEN THIGH AND GRAVY.... but we'll be touching on THAT dish much later in the book..)

I'm moderately lactose intolerant, and about twice a day I'd get a little container of lactose-free milk, for tea and/or cereal. I never used it on the tea... but I could have done with more than one tiny packet of sugar.

I cut off the part of the image where the milk was listed, and where I 'highlighted' it. I was starting to risk not having space to type anything here.

Oh, look. I estimated badly. I have more space. Well. I guess I'd better make use of it with something deep and insightful.

80085 80085 80085 80085 80085 80085. There. You're welcome.

DICED SQUASH**
MASHED POTATO**

CRUSHED PINEAPPLE**

SUGAR**
TEA**

NO?!

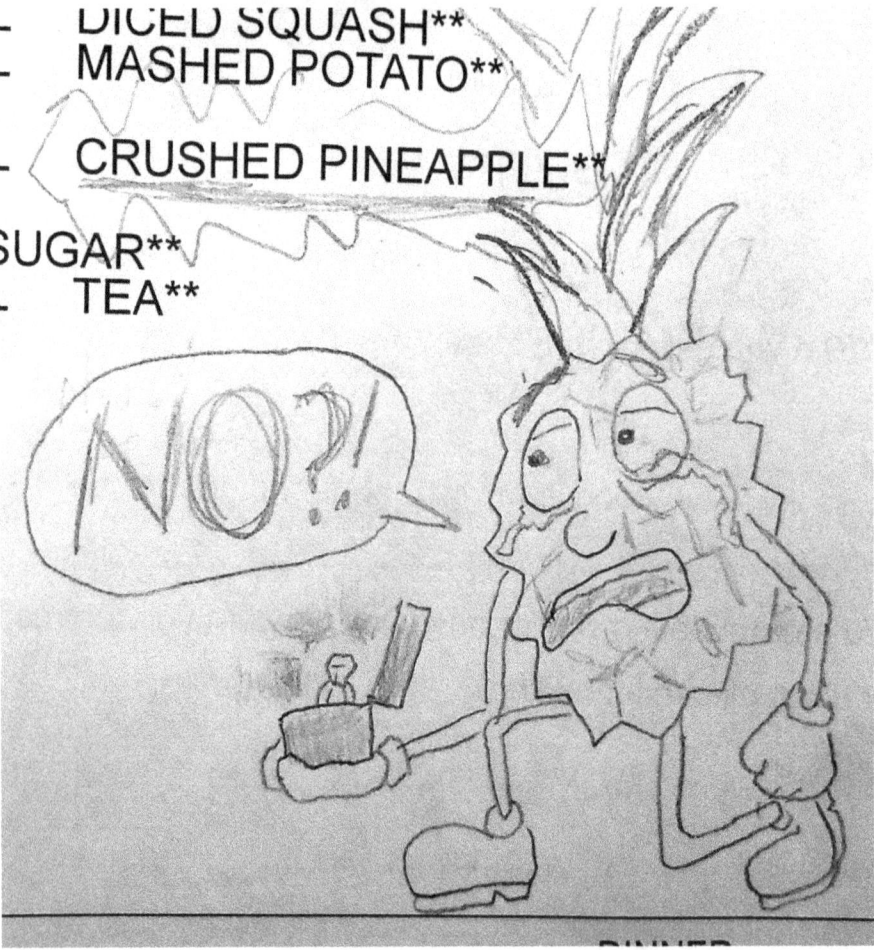

You thought I'd express 'crushed' in a literal, violent way?? Why would you ever think.. Huh. Yeah, I understand.

Kind of off topic, but have you ever heard of a "durian"? Picture a pineapple, possessed by some mid-plane demon. Extra spiky, hard to open without a hatchet, and the STINK when opened! They're banned in a ton of places in regions of Asia (where some brave souls *like* to eat them,) due to the omnipresent, long, long lingering stench.

Ah, but the taste?... Soggy garbage with cigarette butts, really. I can't think of how else to describe it. It's the anti-pineapple. In end times, pineapples and durians will battle for the souls of all the produce.

No, jelly doesn't come in glass jars in the hospital... just little white plastic containers you peel open to reveal this entity that seems to want to be Jell-o.

And see on the list- "English muffin"? I didn't want to doodle that one. A muffin with a monocle, muttonchops and a bowler hat would have been what I'd have done... but... a little too obvious, y'know?

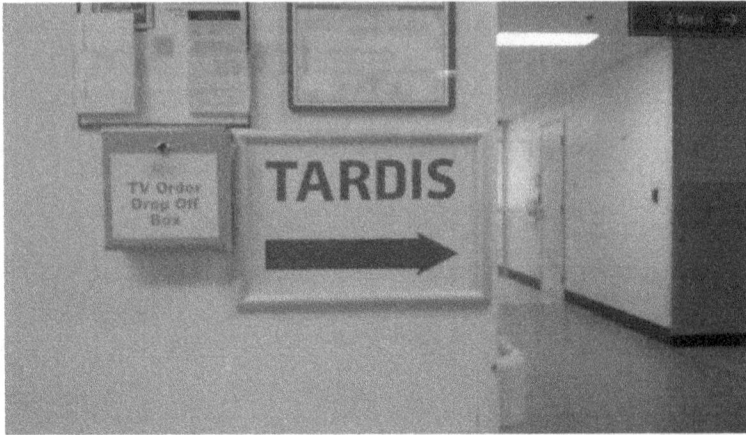

And just for kicks, here's a photo I took in the hospital during my short bursts of freedom from the bed.

I followed the arrow, but didn't find any big blue-box time-machines.

Probably because the sign actually said 'stairs' before I messed it up on the computer. When I saw the sign, it made me instantly think of 'TARDIS' before I'd actually read it.

What? Juvenile? As if the rest of the book is any more mature...

Wanna know a pervy secret? The orange piece here at least has its peel on still. The ones that came on my tray were sans-peel. A little dish of nekkid orange pieces, who'd been doing who-knows-what before I saw them.

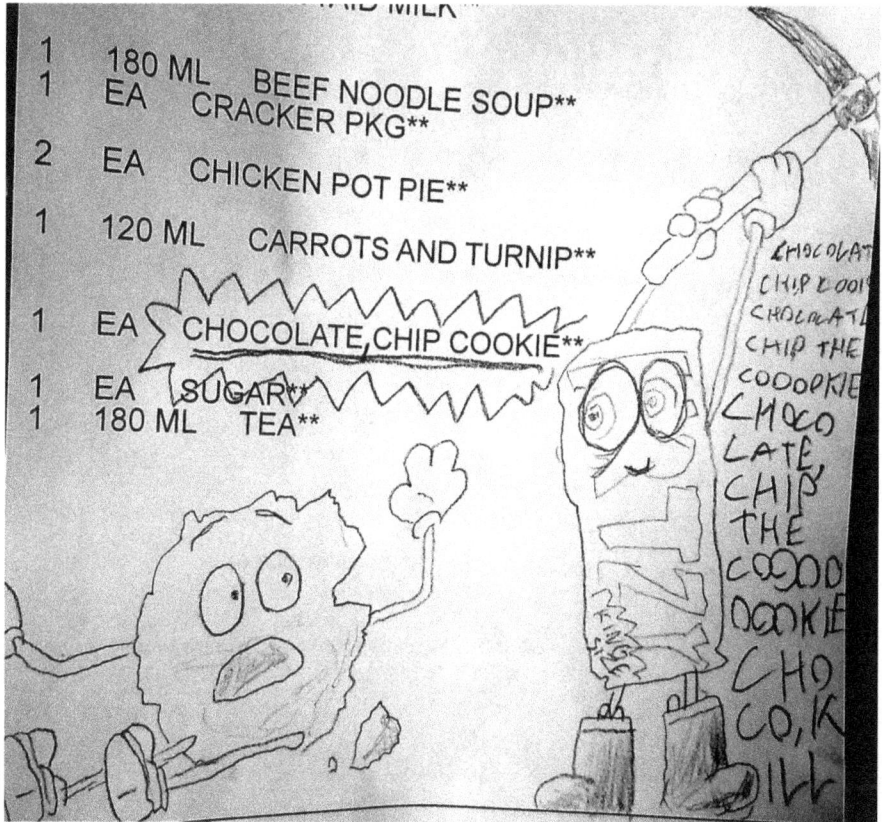

A chocolate bar was hearing voices... evil little comma... chocolate, chip cookie...!

They were good cookies, worth the lactose.

7 PC   RED POTATO WEDGES**
120 ML   ZUCCHINI**

125 ML   APPLESAUCE**

EA   SUGAR**
180 ML   TEA**

Yeah, go ahead, keep calling it a thong. I call it a self-inflicted WEDGIE.

:TR R

At least I didn't draw a human getting a wedgie using a potato. Eh, two more potato-themed ones coming up. You might get lucky yet, spud.

120 ML MASHED SWEET POTATO**
120 ML PEAS**

SLICE CARROT CAKE**

EA SUGAR**
180 ML TEA**

IF I'M SO #?!@ SWEET, WHY MASH ME?

I'm not the biggest fan of sweet potatoes, but repeated exposure during my stay has given me at least a *little* appreciation for them.

I'd rather have normal mashed potatoes, even instant, with enough salty soy sauce to turn it a rich brown...

Shut up, don't call me sick! Try it! I first tried it when I was a kid, and saw a place of 'riced' potatoes coming at me. I was all excited for rice, and grabbed the soy sauce out of the cupboard... then saw... oh.. not rice. SCREW IT! SOY HAS BEEN SUMMONED, SOY SHALL BE USED!

My parents were skeptical. They never joined me in the dark side of the mash.

1   EA   APPLE JUICE**
1   120 ML   COLESLAW**

2   EA   SALISBURY STEAK & GRAVY**
1   120 ML   MASHED POTATO**
1   120 ML   MIXED VEGETABLE**
1   125 ML   DICED PEACHES**

1   EA   SUGAR**
1   180 ML   TEA**

Handwritten: "SPUD-EYE, this steak isn't one of ours, why operate on him?" "This bloody steak needs our help. It Burned. It doesn't matter to me if he's from Salisbury."

Handwritten: "So.... how do I do this without arms?"

Handwritten: MⓐⓢⒽⓔⒹ

Handwritten: (FIRST EVER MASH/ MASHED POTATO PARODY!)

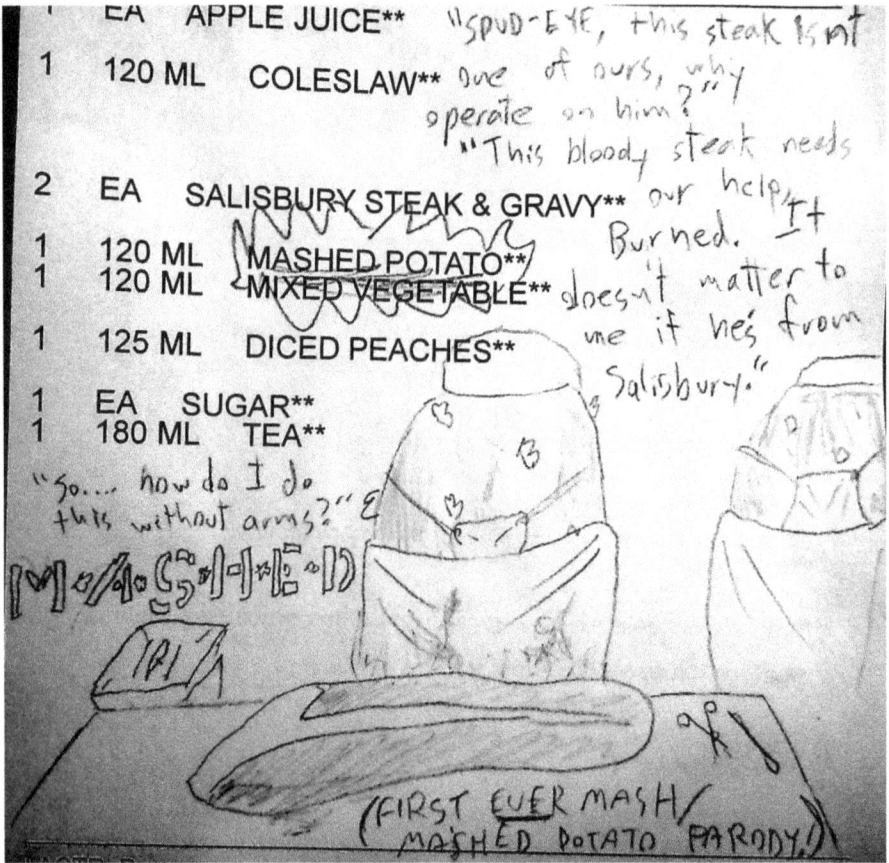

For those who don't know, a Salisbury steak looks nothing like a T-bone. My doodle also looks very little like a T-bone.

As far as I'm concerned, MASH was the best sitcom ever. And Salisbury steak is a hamburger patty that has delusions of grandeur.

I lived in a town called Salisbury for a year or two.
It had *no* delusions of grandeur.

Except that I had a huge outdoor pool. Which gave me, as a kid, my own delusions of grandeur.*

*two year late edit: I'm confusing my towns I lived in. Salisbury didn't have the pool. With luck, maybe Salisbury found a source of grandeur since the last time I was there.

```
1    120 ML    PEAS**
1    120 ML    RICE PILAF**
1    125 ML    MANDARIN ORANGES**
1    EA    SUGAR**
1    180 ML    TEA**
```

Samuri Oranges
of the
Mandarin Empire
HAVE.
HONOUR!
LOYALTY!
VITAMIN C!!!

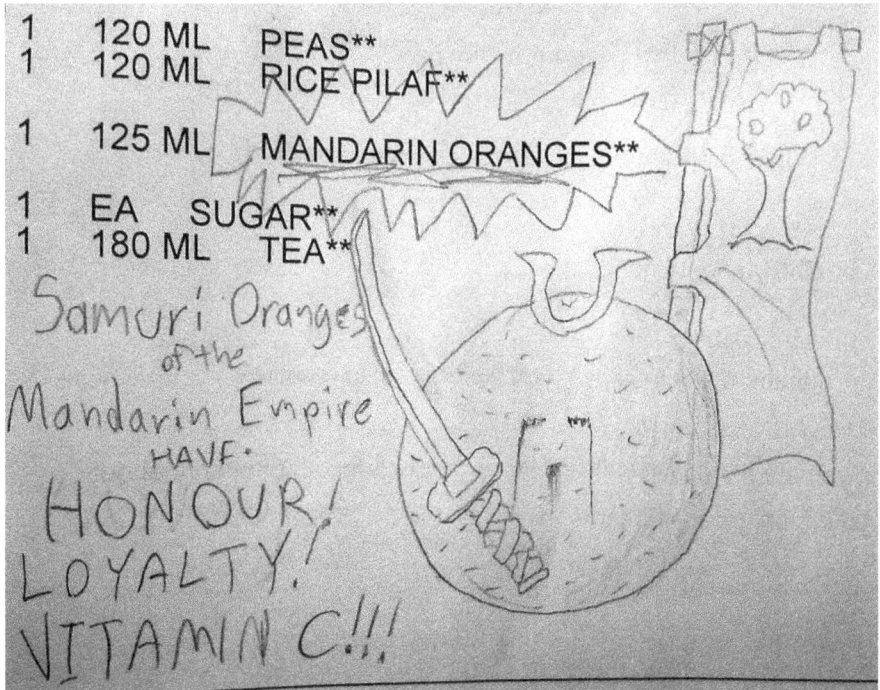

Wow. Look, I misspelled 'samurai'. I could have added the second 'a' with the computer, but I decided to leave it as is, so that you understand the way the medications were affecting me.

What was I on? Calcium, iron, you know... chemicals infamous for creating spelling errors. Right? Right? We all know I'd never slip up otherwise!

WW SALMON SANDWICH**

ML   FRUIT COCKTAIL**

SUGAR**
ML   TEA**

That's right, SALMON sandwich. Everyone knows you get MERCURY from TUNA. I'm hoping for a BMW.

VOTE FOR PEDRO

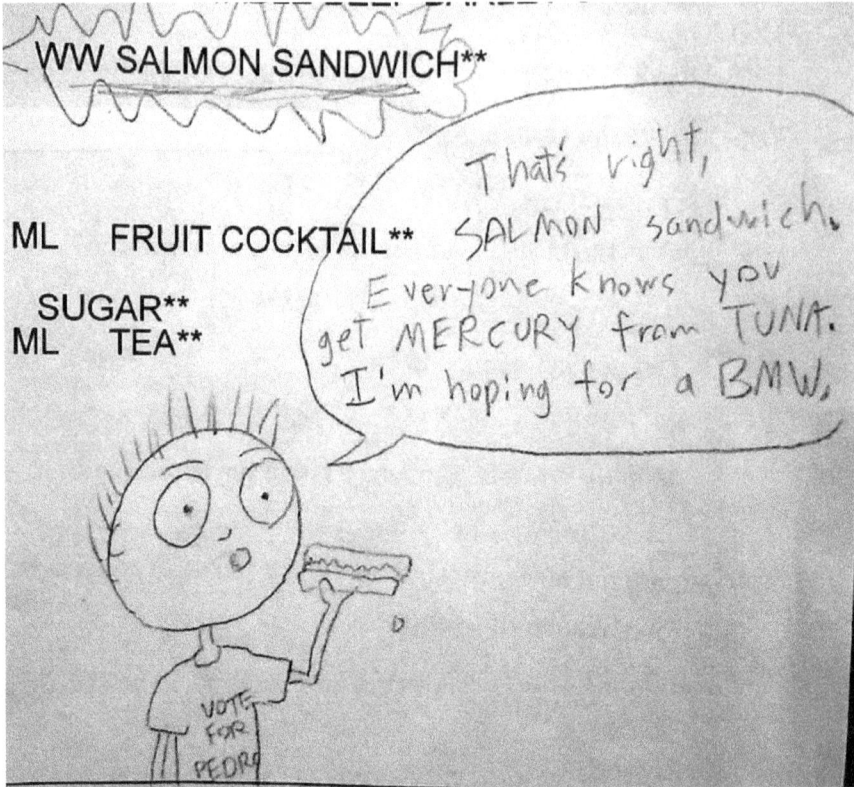

Dang. It just occurred to me... "WW" is what they use to abbreviate "whole wheat". For all the WW items that I had, I never* doodled any of them to mean "World War".

Just think. This one could have been "World War Salmon Sandwich".

Frig, there's a title for a short story at least.

*never until the next visit, read on..

```
 2    180 ML    CHICKEN CACCIATORE**
 1    120 ML    GREEN BEANS**
 1    120 ML    WHITE RICE**
 1    SLICE     APPLE CRUMBLE**
 1    EA    SUGAR**
 1    180 ML    TEA**
```

CHICKEN
CATCH A
TORY

DINNER

From the first time I had chicken cacciatore as a kid, I thought it sounded like "Catch a Tory". Not that I had any clue what a tory was, back then. I don't aim to be overly political here, but maybe the chicken happens to have a dislike (or recipe) for Paul Martin.

Yes, that's supposed to be Paul Martin. This is a fine time to remind you, gentle readers, that all of these drawings were done in a hurry. Quick guide: If you think a drawing is really awful, I was in a big hurry. If you think a drawing of mine is amazing, I was still in a bit of a hurry, but merely managed to summon strength from a fathomless wellspring of talent.

Nothing like *that* appears in this book. And I'd have to check to see if such a fantastic phenomenon has ever occurred at all.

I think once in the 80s.

A lot of awesome stuff happened in the 80s.
I might have done some of it.

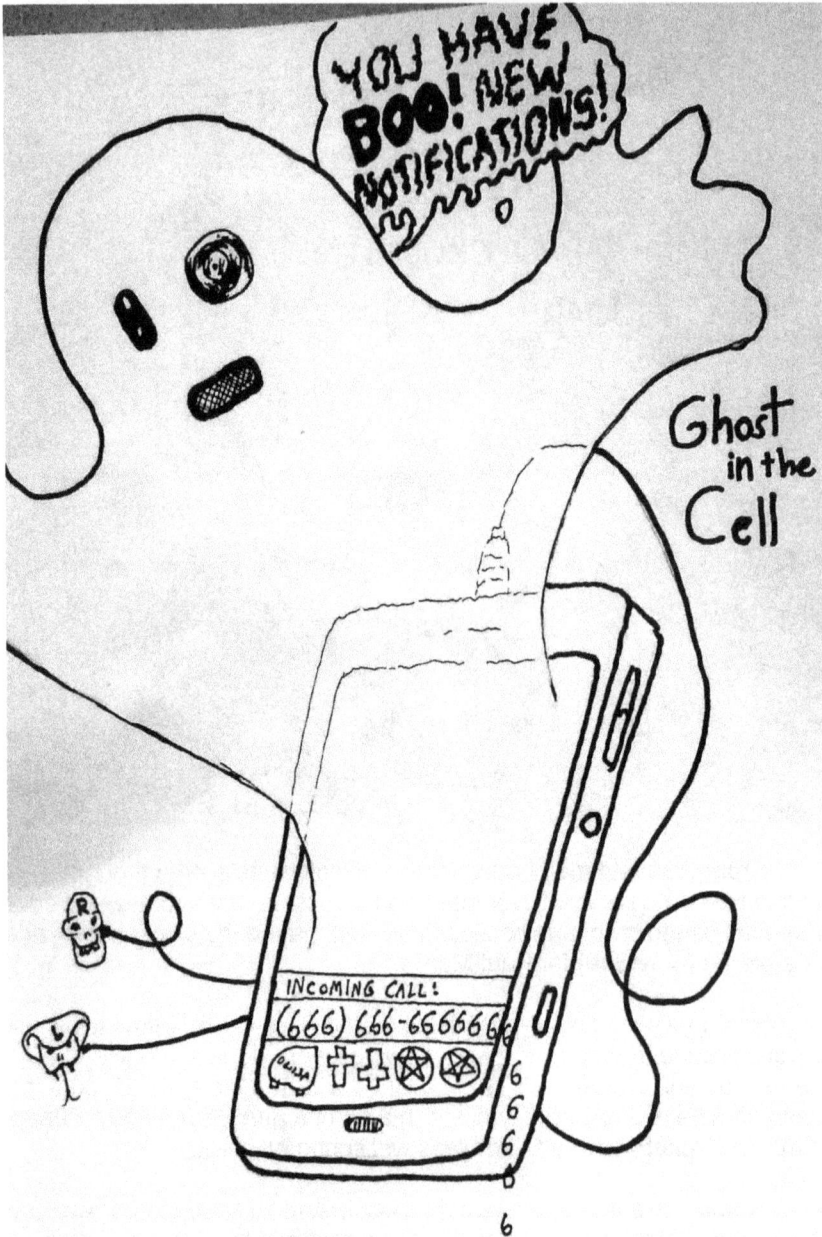

Remember the skeleton in a skirt near the beginning of the book? Yeah. This was drawn around the same time. So here's a little intermission from food doodles. Compared to the food doodles, It took a little more time, effort, a proper sheet of paper, and bothering to actually ink it.

"Ghost in the Cell" is a play on words with one of my fav animes, "Ghost in the Shell". His face is supposed to look like a phone's camera, speaker, etc... The rest of the details are just random haunted silliness.

CRANBERRY JUICE**

LICE   BEET SALAD**

BEAT SALAD!

0 GR   SLICED PORK & GRAVY**

20 ML   PEAS & CARROTS**
20 ML   WHITE RICE**

LICE   CARROT CAKE**

EA   SUGAR**
180 ML   TEA**

DINNER

SUNDAY

19/04/2015

ACTR, R

PICARD, JOSEPH ALFRED
2W-254A

Poor little traumatized salad dressing. Beet salad is evil, seen at the bottom. The salad getting beaten in the doodle looks half decent.

2   120 GR   ROAST BEEF & GRAVY**

1   120 ML   CAULIFLOWER**
1   120 ML   MASHED POTATO**

1   SLICE   CARROT CAKE**

1   EA   SUGAR**
1   180 ML   TEA**

By my daughter's decree,
I have drawn "a roast
beef wearing mashed
potato as a hat."

Hi. It's 'one grapes' again.
this whole plural thing is messing with my mind.
Is a "ROAST BEEF" singular or plural? Or some quantum

LACTR, R

DINNER physics crap?
SUNDAY I never
03/05/2015 learned
         that in school.
              I'M
        PRODUCE.

My daughter had made a suggestion on a doodle about a week before this one, which I forgot, and drew something else on that slip... so when she said I should draw roast beef with mashed potato as a hat... well, I owed her one, who am I to disagree?

Another half-banana one. For those not nerdy enough, the text is mutilated from a pivotal quote from Kirk's eulogy for Spock.

Oops, I misspelled Clarice.

Evidently chicken cannibalism is bad enough, but Fanta makes it worse. Whether Clarice just doesn't like Fanta, or she loves it, and hates to see it paired with cannibalism, who's to say?

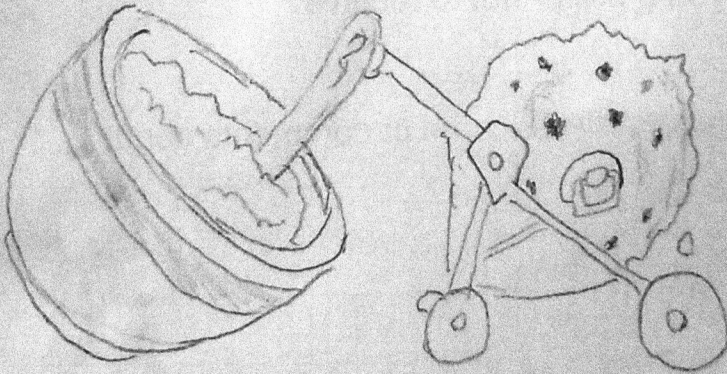

1   EA   OATMEAL RAISIN COOKIE**

1   EA   SUGAR**
1   180 ML   TEA**

OATMEAL, RAISING A COOKIE.

LACTR, R

Oatmeal raisin cookies (which now and then came with lunch,) are one of the few acceptable uses for oatmeal. And now you know the care that goes into making them.

The hospital nutritionist visited me early on, before they tried to serve me oatmeal for breakfast, and got a few of my 'hates' to avoid. Oatmeal, eggs... oh, and lactose is not my friend. (As marked by "LACTR, R" on the slips of paper)- leaving rather few options in the breakfast arena for me.

Muffin and cereal, or English muffin and cereal, repeat, repeat. Now and then a Belgian waffle with some bacon. I was never the world's biggest breakfast fan... and hospital food didn't have much hope of changing that.

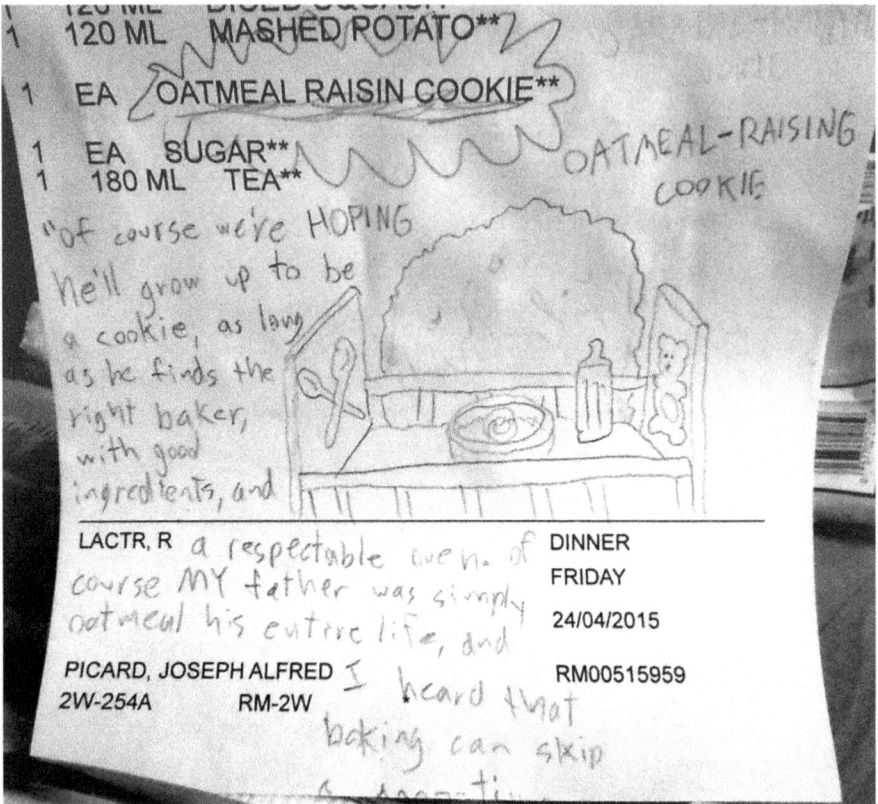

120 ML DICED...
1 120 ML   MASHED POTATO**
1 EA   OATMEAL RAISIN COOKIE**
1 EA   SUGAR**
1 180 ML TEA**

OATMEAL-RAISING
COOKIE

"of course we're HOPING
he'll grow up to be
a cookie, as long
as he finds the
right baker,
with good
ingredients, and

LACTR, R   a respectable oven. of   DINNER
course MY father was simply   FRIDAY
oatmeal his entire life, and   24/04/2015

PICARD, JOSEPH ALFRED I   RM00515959
2W-254A   RM-2W   heard that
                 baking can skip

Oatmeal-raising cookie. Yeah...so... A little punctuation paints a different story, yeah? Sunriiiise, sunset...

We all know a cookie will go on and on about their kids if you let 'em.

Huh? Your cookies don't talk? Try making them at home, and not just getting them from the store.

EA   CORN FLAKES

EA   PEANUT BUTTER**

EA   MARGARINE**
EA   STRAWBERRY JAM**
EA   WW   ENGLISH MUFFIN**

EA   SUGAR**
180 ML   TEA

STRAWBERRY JAM SESSION

HEY, MAN, IF WE DON'T GET A GIG SOON, OUR CAREER IS TOAST.

For all the jam that found me at breakfast, I almost always shunned it for the peanut butter... Peanut butter has all that nutty protein that helps heal the wound.

-If you can assume that the typical big brand fakie peanut butter has much in it that's any good for you. I've been mostly converted to natural peanut butter at home, despite the pile of oil you're supposed to stir in, and how runny it is... (tip: drain out half the oil as soon as you open it the first time. Despite my wife's fears, you don't end up with a hard, unmanageable mess by the end of the jar.)

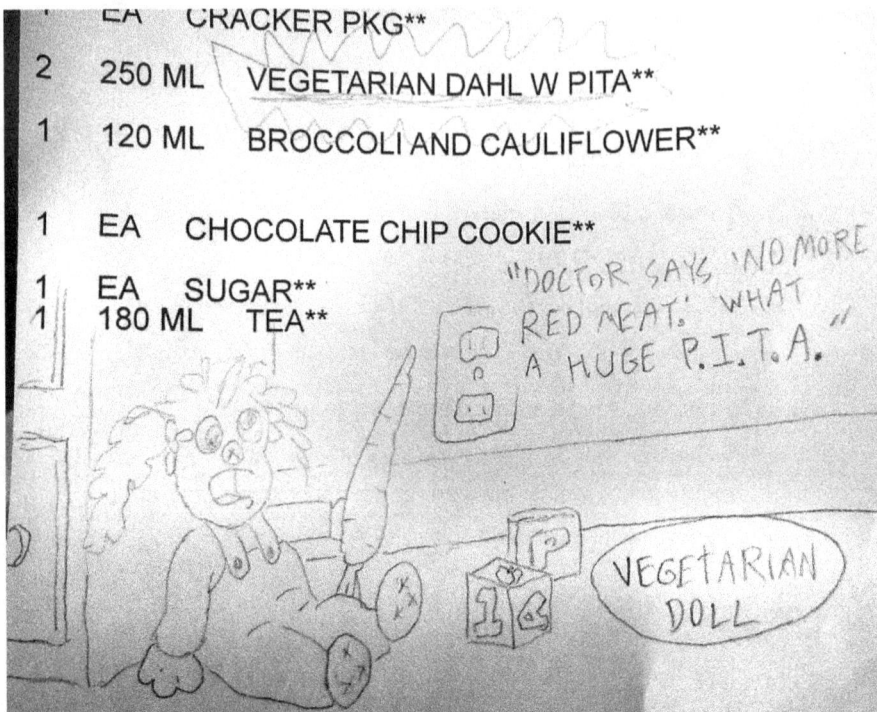

Being an uncultured slob, I'd never heard of dahl before. Hm... and now, I can't remember what it was. My uncultured nature is resilient to learning new things!

...yay?

I was considering making the doll "Chuckie", But I suspect he's too bloodthisrty to be a vegetarian.

"Resource 2.0" (made by Cadbury* of all things) is a non-dairy milkshake-thing that they had me drinking every morning. It was meant to increase my protein intake, for the sake of healing. They... weren't awful.

Why does the slip mention "ORAL" with it? I wasn't going to take it through any other holes in my body. I mean, it comes in a juice-like tetra pack with a straw. Which doesn't hook up to the I.V. very well at all.

*In view of the water-privatization nonsense that Cadbury has been up to, many calls for boycotting them have passed through the hallowed halls of Facebook. I would have joined a boycott, but upon looking at all the stuff Cadbury makes, I had seemingly been pre-cotting them.

Then I get presented a Cadbury product to help me heal. (I found this out by reading the fine print on the side of the container) Ehhh... I put my pre-cott aside for a month and a half or so. Yay for convictions! And NOW there's droughts going on in California. Oops.

EA BEEF & PORK CABBAGE ROLLS**

1	120 ML	GREEN BEANS**
1	120 ML	WHITE RICE**
1	SLICE	NANAIMO BAR**
1	EA	SUGAR**
1	180 ML	TEA**

CABBAGE? SHIVER ME TIMBERS I'M @!?#ED NOW!

CABB

LACTR, R

DINNER
THURSDAY

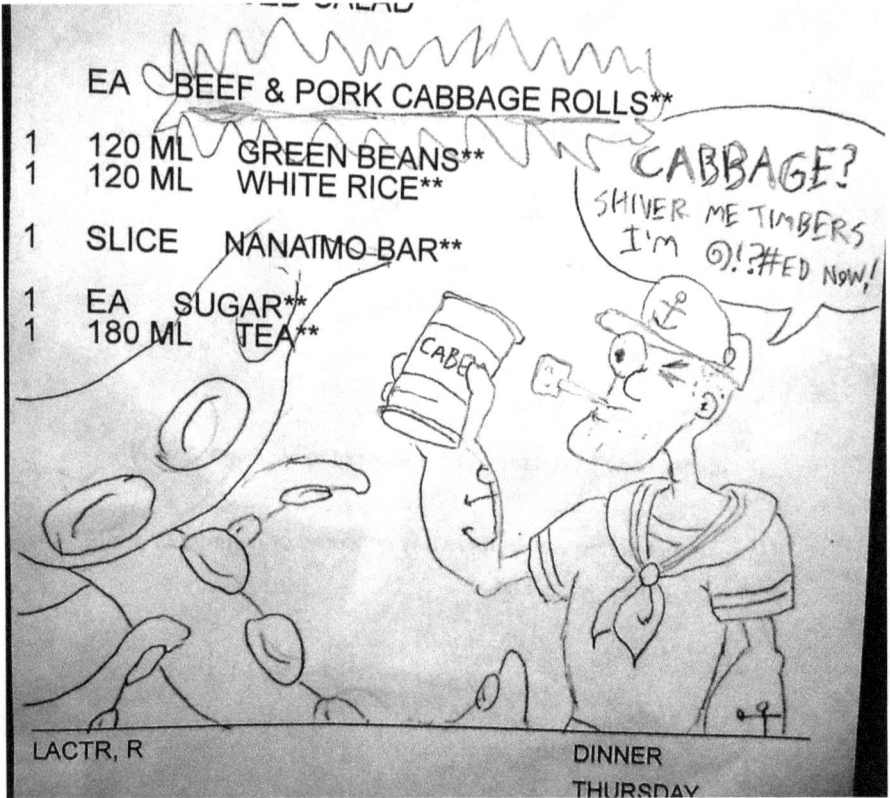

Back in elementary school, I could draw a pretty darned good Popeye. And I charged a nickle for pictures. I think I lost my knack... this guy looks like a skinny younger brother to Popeye. Like Luigi is to Mario.

For the record... cabbage rolls? Ew. I quickly found out I could make a quick little incision, and neatly get out the beef & pork... uh.. stuffing? loaf? --out of the middle, making this meal salvageable to I, a cabbage hater.

```
1  EA  GRAPES**

1  EA  SUGAR**
1  180 ML  TEA**
```

MLT

MAJOR LEAGUE TEA

"ML TEA."
MLT... ya?

Shush, I thought it was funny. And because I have a lot of tea-loving friends, I did the following...

MLT

MAJOR LEAGUE TEA

Yeah, now available as a T-shirt. The MLT T.

http://ozero.spreadshirt.ca/major-league-tea-t-A101952727 it's there, and a handful of others. --unless this book survives my spreadshirt account. Huh.

If you can't click that, just google up "Major League Tea" in quotes, and you should get the link.

Unless the internet just eats the shirt, instead.

Huh.

1 HALF BANANA** HALF HORSE**

1 EA SUGAR** BANANTAUR

1 180 ML TEA**

I SEE A BRIGHT FUTURE FOR YOU, MODELING FOR THE COVERS of BAD ROMANCE NOVELS.

SILKO.

LUNCH

LACTR, R

SATURDAY

09/05/2015

This is the final "half banana" doodle. He's no Fabio, but some ladies really like horses. Ask Catherine the Great. Tog doesn't seem to be into it.

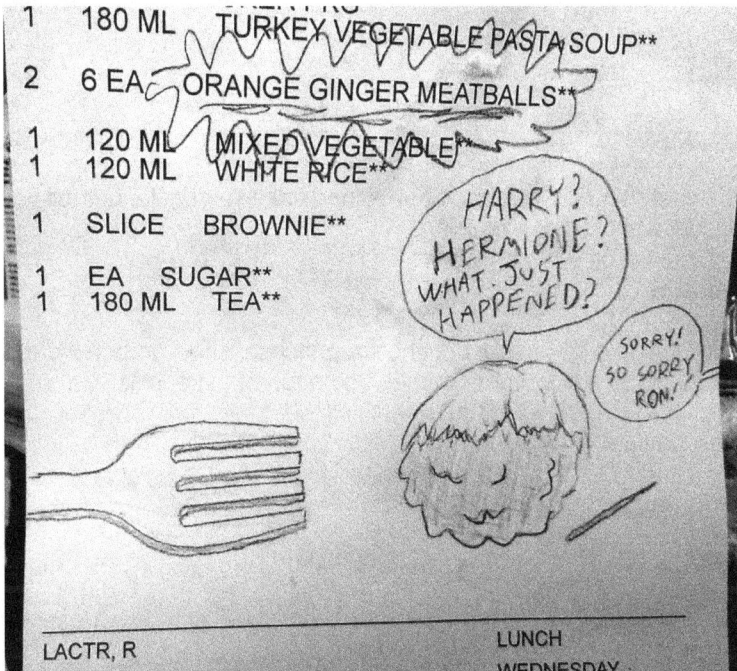

1 180 ML TURKEY VEGETABLE PASTA SOUP**

2 6 EA ORANGE GINGER MEATBALLS**

1 120 ML MIXED VEGETABLE**

1 120 ML WHITE RICE**

1 SLICE BROWNIE**

1 EA SUGAR**

1 180 ML TEA**

HARRY? HERMIONE? WHAT JUST HAPPENED?

SORRY! SO SORRY RON!

LUNCH

LACTR, R

WEDNESDAY

There. Much more polite meatballs than earlier. Um... depending on who you blame for Ron's situation.

And see that brownie on the list? ... another rogue agent slipping through my lactose ban.

CRANBERRY JUICE**

1   120 ML   COLESLAW**

HELLO PRINCESS PEACH.
I WANT TO PLAY A
GAME....

2   120 GR   SLICED PORK & GRAVY**

1   120 ML   PRINCE EDWARD MEDLEY**
1   120 ML   WHITE RICE**

1   125 ML   DICED PEACHES**

MARIO!!

1   EA   SUGAR**
1   180 ML   TEA**

SAVE ME!!!...AGAIN.

CHOP-O-MATIC

CHOP!

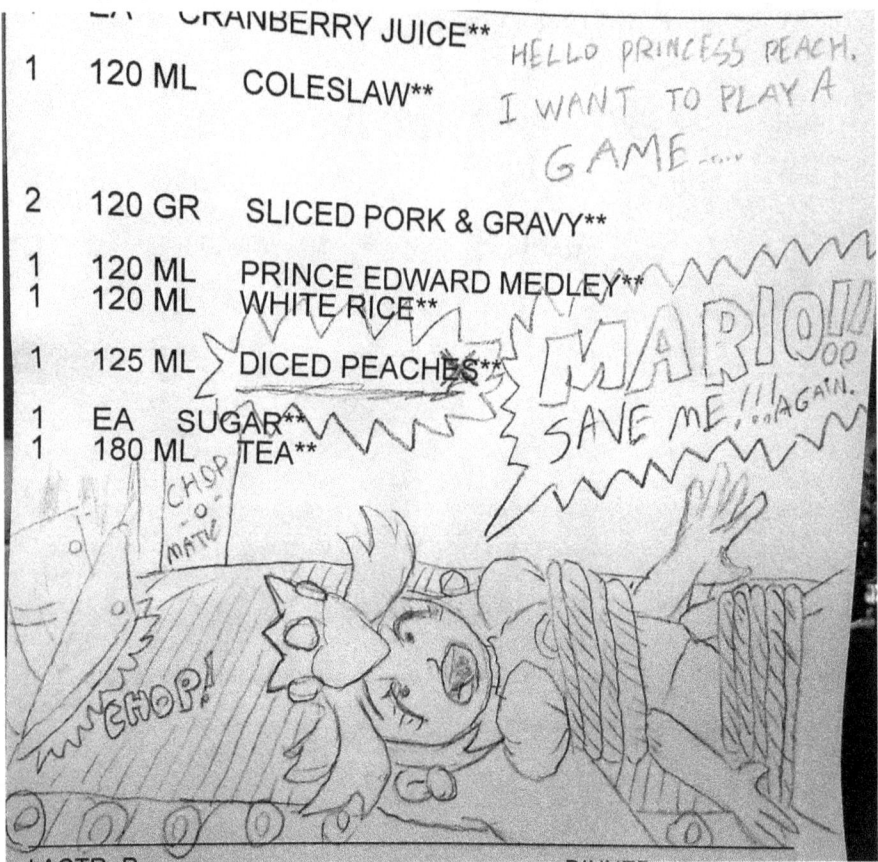

Oh, what? You smile when I make food talk like people, but roll your eyes when I just want to eat people?

Hypocrite.

Okay, this is a bit grizzly, but she's a princess, she's gotta have a bajillion coins, which translates in her games into a ton of extra lives.

She'll be fine.

Honest.

Or if she isn't, she'll just respawn at the start of the level, or the world map, or whatever, depending on what neighbourhood she's in.

2 EA KRUNCHY PERCH & TARTAR SAUCE**

1 120 ML DICED CARROTS**
1 120 ML RICE PILAF**

1 EA GRAPES**

1 EA SUGAR**
1 180 ML TEA**

IN THE END...
THERE CAN BE
ONLY ONE!!

(GRAPES)

WASN'T
IT A "PERCH" JOKE
TODAY? YOU HAD
LIKE 4 TURNS
NOW, NO-ONE'S
A HIGHLANDER

THE
ONE
GRAPES
WILL
RETURN
IN!

ONLY
ONE!!

LACTR, R

THE ONE
GRAPES:
RELOADED
...COMING SOON

LUNCH
TUESDAY
05/05/2015

Yeah, Tog had a little breakdown over his 'singular/plural' issues.

And the Krunchy Perch... No allusions to the klan there, I think it was breaded with a mix featuring Special K. Shut up, it was kinda good, and I'm not generally a fish fan.

SHEPHERD'S PIE & GRAVY**

1   120 ML   PEAS**

1   125 ML   FRUIT COCKTAIL**

1   EA   SUGAR**
1   180 ML   TEA**

"You goin' to the bar after shift, sarge?"

"WHAT? Rookie, we're going there NOW, for lunch!"

"Sarge, it's 10 A.M."

". . . ."

"and?"

LACTR, R   LUNCH

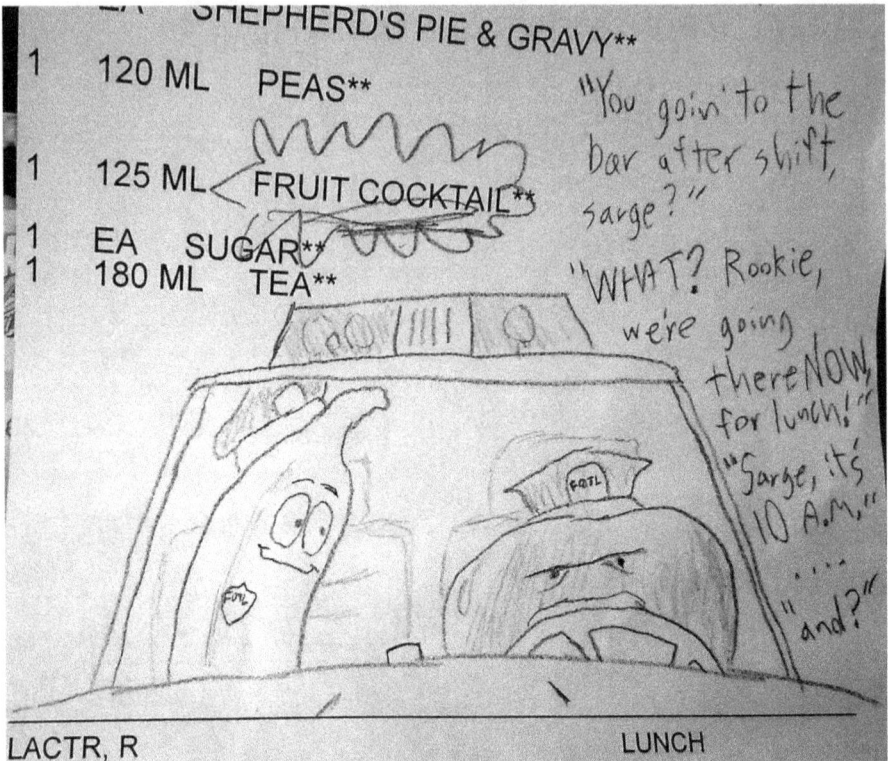

Okay, the cocktail stretch to 'bar' is a little thin, but who cares? If ended up a fun little comic.

And it's even hard to see on the original paper, but the badges say "FOTL"

Which of course stands for Fruit of the LAW.

A   RICE KRISPIES**

A   PEANUT BUTTER**

A   MARGARINE**
A   STRAWBERRY JAM**
A   WW / ENGLISH MUFFIN**

A   SUGAR**
80 ML   TEA

RIGHT, THEN. IS THIS ONE MORE FOR THE ROAD? CHEERS, THEN, AND THANK YE KINDLY FOR ALL YA LOT DONE. NOW THEN, I EXPECT THEY BE WAITIN' FOR ME AT HOME. SAFE TRAVELS, THE LOT OF YA.

R, R   BREAKFAST

FINE, fine, I'll do the English muffin. Just like I said. Monocle, twirled mustache, bowler hat.
And a brew for good measure.

This was my parting message to the kitchen staff. As I wrote this, all the ducks were lined up for me to go home at last.

My thanks go to all the kitchen staff for putting up with me, the doctors for getting things on the right track, and of course, of course, the amazing nursing staff.
I've seen and heard nurses putting up with things beyond the job description, (such as the slimy pirate ******* -- long story I'm not at liberty to share with the general public)
Thanks to the whole hospital, and community support people, friends and family, getting me through all of this.

But I'm very ready for non-hospital food.

Oh... was I saying goodbye to the hospital?

#notsofastpunk

There was a delay in setting up home for my still-not-fully-healed self. A minor thing. One more night here, huh? More hospital food, which means... two more doodles after this, if inspiration strikes.

EA APPLE JUICE**
1 EA ITALIAN DRESSING** LAST ONE!
1 EA TOSSED SALAD** -- I'M PRETTY SURE...

2 EA BEEF & PORK CABBAGE ROLLS** THANKS AGAIN,
FOLKS!
1 120 ML PEAS**
1 120 ML WHITE RICE**

1 SLICE BUTTER TART BAR**

1 EA SUGAR**
1 180 ML TEA**

DUDE, WHAT'S YOUR BEEF WITH SALADS?

-GRRRR...

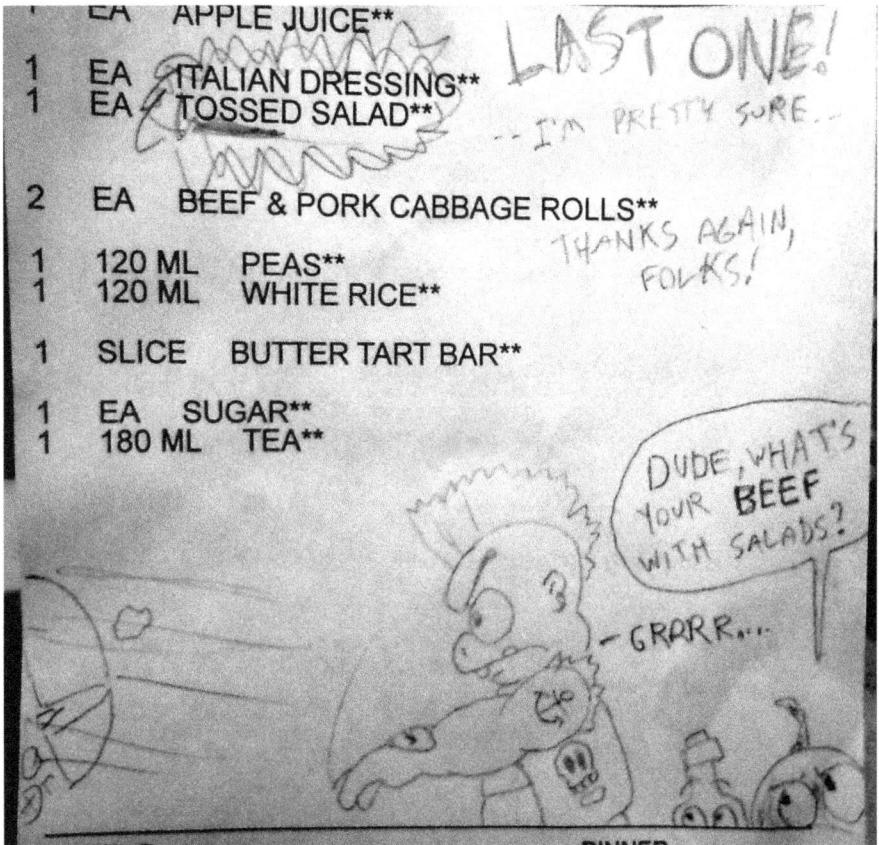

Dinner on my last full day here. I already got a little sappy on the breakfast one, so it felt silly to be overly sappy this time... but as I was finishing this doodle, Linda came by. It seemed a little too soon to be collecting my tray. She gave me a card and said thanks for all the doodles, and so on. She went to attend to duties, and I hurried to wrap up the doodle, and find my phone to take the picture.

I couldn't find my phone, and mid-panic, I realized it was probably in the pocket on my wheelchair which was clear across the room. (I'd been in it for my allotted two hours earlier.) I rang the buzzer to call a nurse, searching everywhere I could reach for my phone in case I was wrong about it being with the chair. The nurse came, found the phone. Panic subsiding... I take the shot...!

With mission accomplished before my tray and doodle were picked up, I could *then* take the time to open the card.

I wasn't expecting the card to begin with. I figured two or three signatures...

I found *sixteen*. With notes, and thanks for the doodles. I was barely manly enough not to cry. One of them even doodled in a little One Grapes, with a bowtie. I think they liked the doodles.

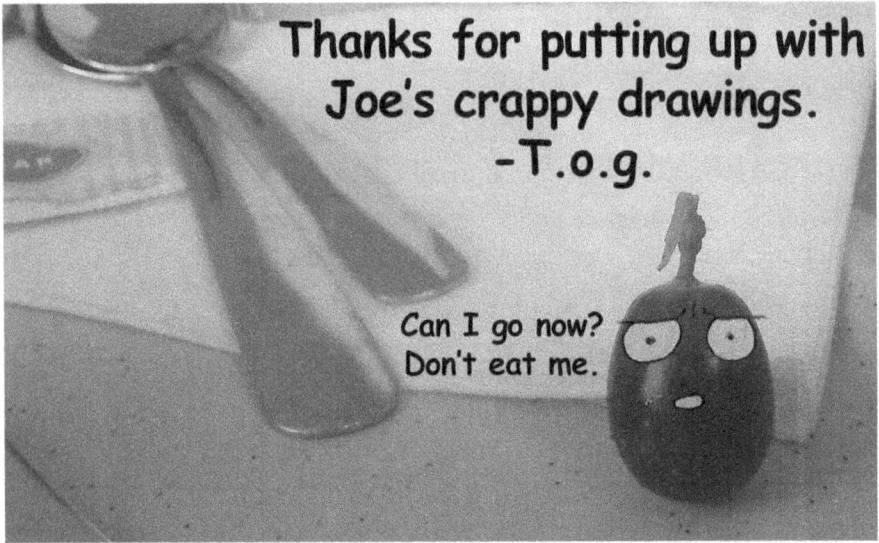

Thanks for putting up with
Joe's crappy drawings.
-T.o.g.

Can I go now?
Don't eat me.

Bye folks! I hope you liked my goofy experiment. Stay out of hospitals, be safe and healthy instead.

And if you *have* to be in a hospital, be nice to the nurses, kind to the staff, and give that tray of hospital food a chance.

THE 2017 STAY

Guess what? There's a new addition to the menu!

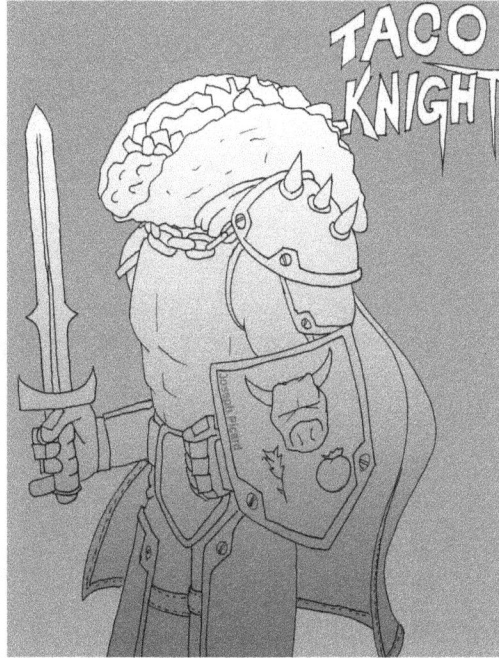

-And tacos are not it. Haven't you learned yet? I shudder to think how a taco would turn out under these dietary regulations. First of all, no cheese for me, lactose. The beef would not be seasoned, at least not in the way we'd want, so... loose burger with .. unsalted gravy? And the salsa? I don't think mild salsa would be mild enough.

You get the idea. So why did I put this guy here? One more excuse to draw something with a bit of detail to show you I can, when not rushed. Okay, if I really wanted to impress, he'd be full colour and shaded nicely, but the book is printed in B&W, so it would be totally lost on you unless you got the e-book. That's right... there's colour photos in here that you can see in the ebook version. Like... 5 of them! Such dramatic photos as actual grapes, and bananas! Now you can only guess what colour those bananas are! They could be purple! Who's to say they aren't?! Not those fuddy-duddies with their books stained on dead tree guts!

Anyway, I've said what there is to say about how I ended up back in the hospital back in the forward by the start of the book, let's get on with it already! (So much for that dramatic farewell on the previous page, huh?)

GRAIN TOAST**
E**
RY JAM**

E**

THE ONE
GRAPES IS
BACK!

- - - -

YAY?

This was my first doodle, on the first breakfast. I was still in the E.R. at this point. I intended this to be an announcement aimed at the kitchen staff, at least any who were here two years ago, and might remember my doodles.

The E.R. nurse who cleared my tray threw the paper out before leaving the room. I assume she's been fired for the offence.

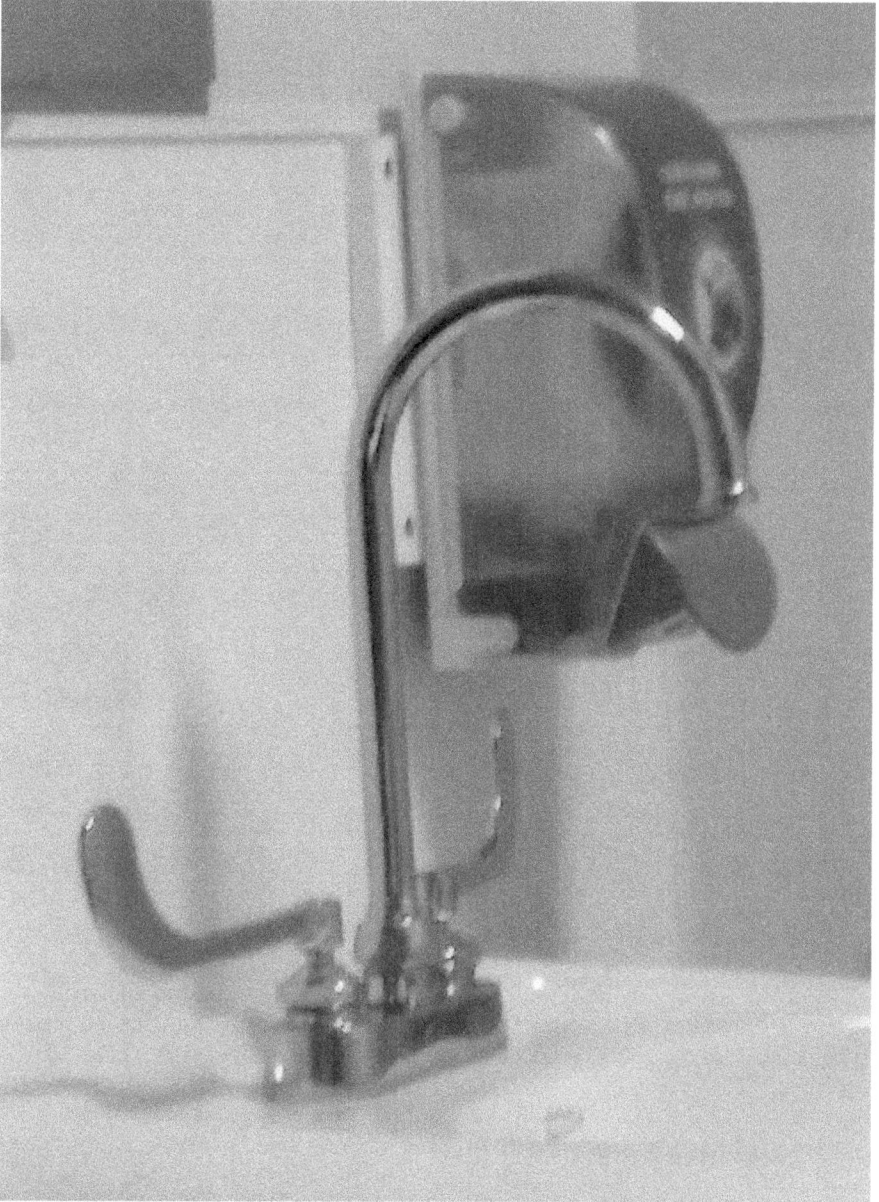

From where I lay,
that fateful day.
I saw this duck.
Well what the ... heck.

You see it too, right? With the little metal wings spread near the bottom, and the soap handle as the bill... Hey. I was bored already, okay? This was in my room in the E.R. Before I was completely admitted. Me stuck in a stretcher, my phone, and no WiFi. That's right. Zero WiFi in this hospital.

EA   CRACKER PKG**

295 ML   CHICKEN CHWDER WW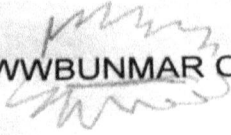BUNMAR CHSE**

SLICE   TRIPLEBERRY CRUMBLE**

A   MILKER**
A   SUGAR**
O ML   TEA BAG/HOT WATER**

My move last year involved a lot of Ikea. We assembled the kitchen cabinets ourselves. Know how Lego kits have simple ones with like 10 pieces for little kids, and huge kits with a billion little pieces for the masochists?

Ikea follows a similar pattern. And instructions with little to no words, and lots of pictures.

And a proportionate frequency of profanity.

This was the moment I realized the food would be 99% the same as two years ago. This slip had a particularly common load of of food. Given my lactose intolerance, aversion to eggs and oatmeal, that left a pretty narrow assortment of things that would find me for breakfast.

Like toast. Like a single slice of soft, pale, choke-resistant toast, alone on a big beveled plate/bowl hybrid with a cover. That wasn't the whole breakfast, there was other stuff on the tray, but lifting the cover of the plate to see one anemic, lonely piece of warmed bread has been a surreal experience.

Almost as surreal as when I lift the cover, and nothing is there... because a muffin has stuck to the cover, and remains momentarily hidden by it.

3...
  2...
    1...

... MUFFIN BOMB!

It drops while you're staring at the apparently empty plate, but before you do anything other than hold the cover up. Thankfully, all of my muffin bombs have landed on the plate, and not onto the edge of the tray, to bounce to the floor and roll away.

EA... GOURMET SALMON SAL ON GRAIN BUI

125 ML   APRICOT HALVES**

EA   SUGAR**
180 ML   TEA BAG/HOT WATER**

NO KELP FOR YOU!!!

OK.

Sandwiches are not uncommon fare, often lunch thrice a week or so, but the *gourmet* salmon sandwich was *different*. It came in a fancy-ish bun, left open, and an ice-cream scoop sized ball of gourmet salmon salad. Which includes cucumber chunks, tiny strings of carrot, and red pepper bits.. I rate these additions in order, as welcome, worthless, and invasive.

I'd take a non-gourmet tuna, quite happily. Cucumbers welcome. Pickles no. People who put pickles in tuna sandwiches are sleeper agents of terrorists, or of 80s coldwar Russians. Or aliens.

Xenex UV robot

Meet Violet. That's a nickname the staff here gave this ultra-violet-spewing thing that gets brought into a room. Everyone is evacuated, and it fries the room of germs. It has a schedule, and I think is scheduled to work a few rooms a day across the hospital.

Excluding my first night in the E.R., I've been in two rooms during my stay, and both have been invaded by Violet, requiring me to be taken to another room, bed and all, rolled elsewhere for a bit.

Violet has been working here for about 8 months, and I'm not about to tell her that she's getting canned this month. She leaves behind a very bleachy smell that irritates a lot of people (I'm not sure how THAT works), her beams are a *cancer* risk for anyone that might walk in on her while she's doin her thing, and she's expensive. I guess she's just a rental.

And yes, she's just about the same size as R2D2. So... think of her as R2D2 that farts bleach, and can give you cancer by staring at you if you walk in on her during her private time.

And I'm SO adding her into a short story I've had on the back burner with a lot of robots in it...

1   EA   ORANGE JUICE**

WANT MORE BEEF TIPS? FINE. 1) NEVER EAT THE BROWN "APPLES". 2) THE DOG IS MORE AFRAID OF US. 3) THE FARMER DID NOT TAKE OLE' BESSIE DOWNSTATE TO LIVE IN A NICE SUBURB.

1   90 GR   BEEF TIPS IN SAUCE**

1   120 ML   PRINCE EDWARD MEDLEY**
1   100 GR   ROASTED PARMESAN POTATO**

1   125 ML   PINEAPPLE TIDBITS**

1   EA   SUGAR**
1   180 ML   TEA BAG/HOT WATER**

More tips from cows! This dish isn't as good as I remember from 2 years ago. Ehhh, still pretty good in the arena of hospital food, though.

180 ML MINESTRONE SOUP**
OPEN HOT BEEF SW ON WW & GRAVY**

120 ML PEAS & CARROTS**

I 125 ML MANDARIN ORANGES**

I EA SUGAR**
I 180 ML TEA BAG/HOT WATER**

"HOT BEEF" SINGLE WOMAN SEEKS WHITE WOMAN WITH GRAVY. MANDARIN A PLUS.

JEEZ, DATING GOT COMPLICATED.

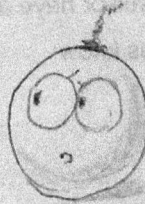

CLASSIFIED
FIND UR ♡

We won't discuss why she calls herself 'hot beef'. It's a code, I'm sure. None of my business. You do you, Beefy. OOOOHHHHHH, I bet she works out a lot.

Ironically, I suppose, I haven't been getting many grapes during this stay. Like... twice in three months? I don't know if this means anything... but you'll notice a lot of doodles involving bananas or banana cake. Was there a coup in the last 2 years?

My thoughts and prayers go out to the missing grapes. May they return safely so I can eat them.

Or not so safely, so I can drink them.

Whenever a nurse asks me if they can get me anything, I've been asking for WiFi and vodka.

I think they think I'm joking.

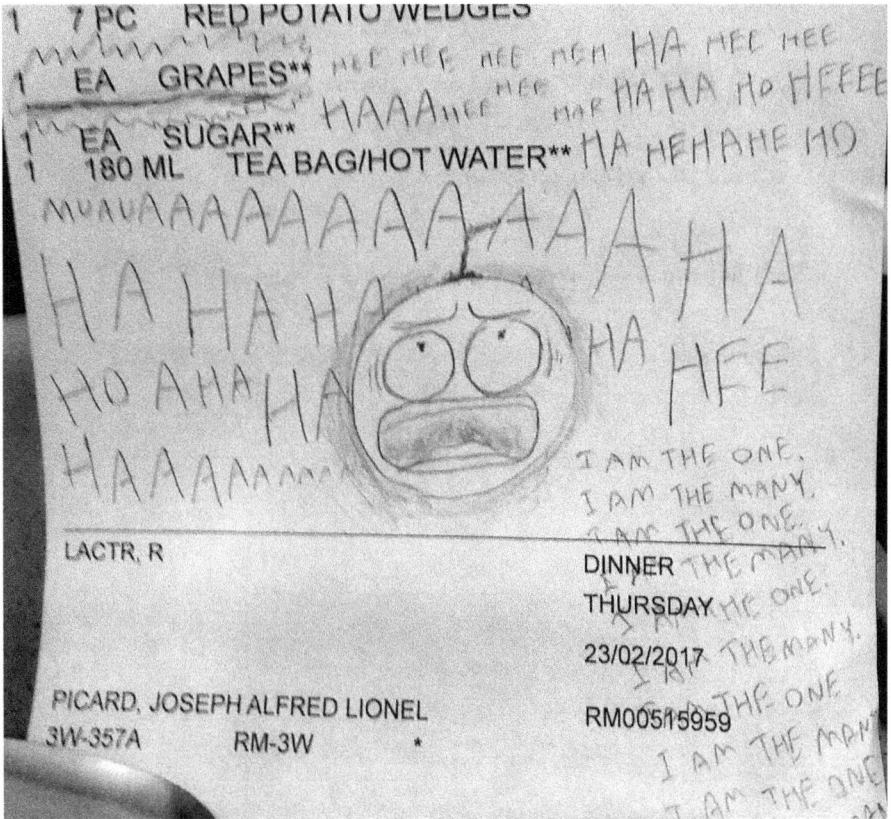

I mean, look at Tog here. He's wracked with worry. He could use a drink.

Probably not the fermented blood of his kin, though. I wonder if he has any attachment to potatoes?

(And yes, as soon as I did this doodle, I had a feeling it would be the basis for the cover. Or a t-shirt. Or a prog-punk band.)

VEGETARIAN CHANA MASALA**

1   120 ML   GREEN BEANS**

1   125 ML   APPLE SLICES**

1   EA   SUGAR**
1   180 ML   TEA BAG/HOT WATER**

THIS IS A REDACTED DOCUMENT???
CONSPIRACY! I KNEW IT! THE
MOON LANDING WAS ALL SOME KIND
OF GOVERNMENT PROJECT! AND THE
MASALA WAS PLEASANTLY SPICY! NOT
OVERLY SO, BUT NOTICABLY! IT MUST
BE A COVERT CALL FOR HELP FROM
LACTR, R THE KITCHEN! HAVE   LUNCH
THEY BEEN OCCUPIED BY   FRIDAY
GOVERNMENT MOON MEN???   24/02/2017
SOMEONE   THE ARMY!
PICARD, JOSEPH ALFRED LIONEL   RM00515959
W-357A   RM-3W OH NO! THEY WORK FOR THE
                GOVERNMENT TOO???

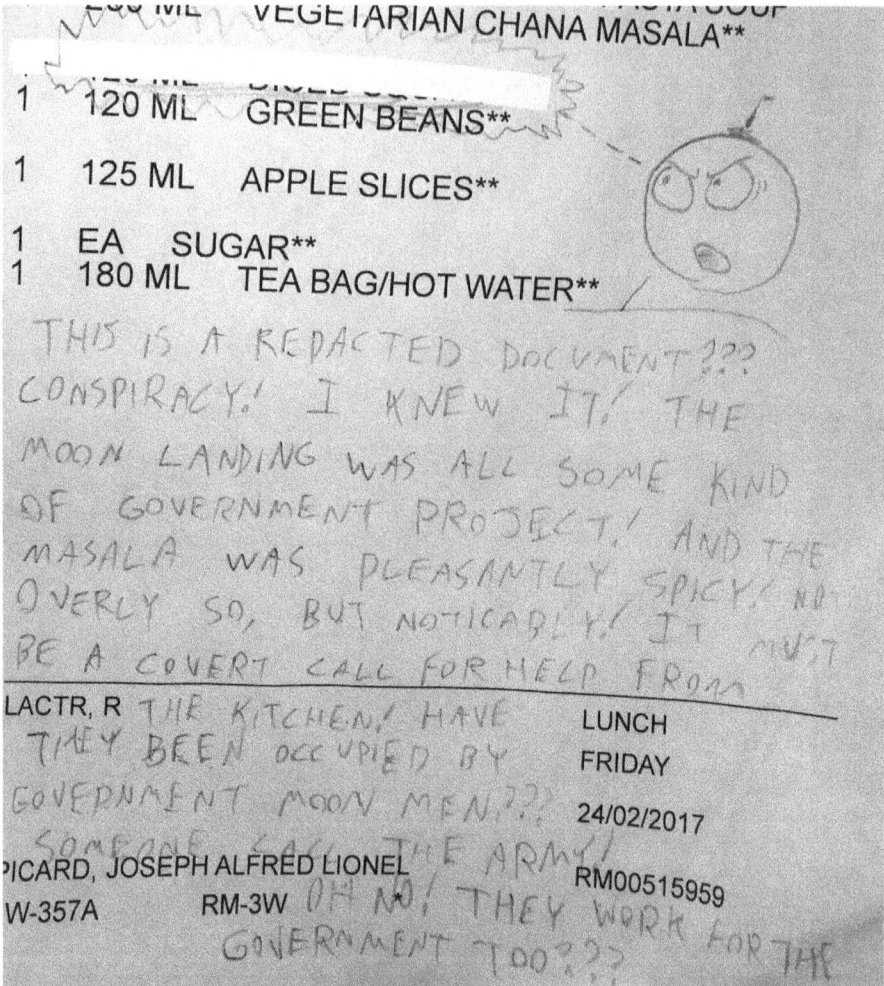

On my last visit, I don't recall seeing any redacted lines on the meal slips. If held to the light just right, you can see what you're missing.

Once, it was erased salad dressing, with a meal that had no salad. That makes a kind of sense. I guess.

But missing potato salad? The motivation is all too clear. More on that later...

EA   BLUEBERRY JAM**
EA   DRY MULTIGRAIN TOAST**
EA   MARGARINE**

EA   SUGAR**
180 ML   TEA BAG/HOT WATER

AHEM, YYYES, THIS
TOAST IS QUITE DRY.
HOW MUCH VERMOUTH
IS IN THIS? .....

...REALLY...
        THAT'S DISAPPOINTING.
  #SAD

Again, the embargo on alcohol impacts my recovery. No vodka, no vermouth, even the ginger beer that I got so often last time has been all but absent. Yes, it was non alcoholic ginger beer, but that only furthers my point.

For the record... by the time I got out of the hospital last time... my interest in ginger beer was pretty much slaked.

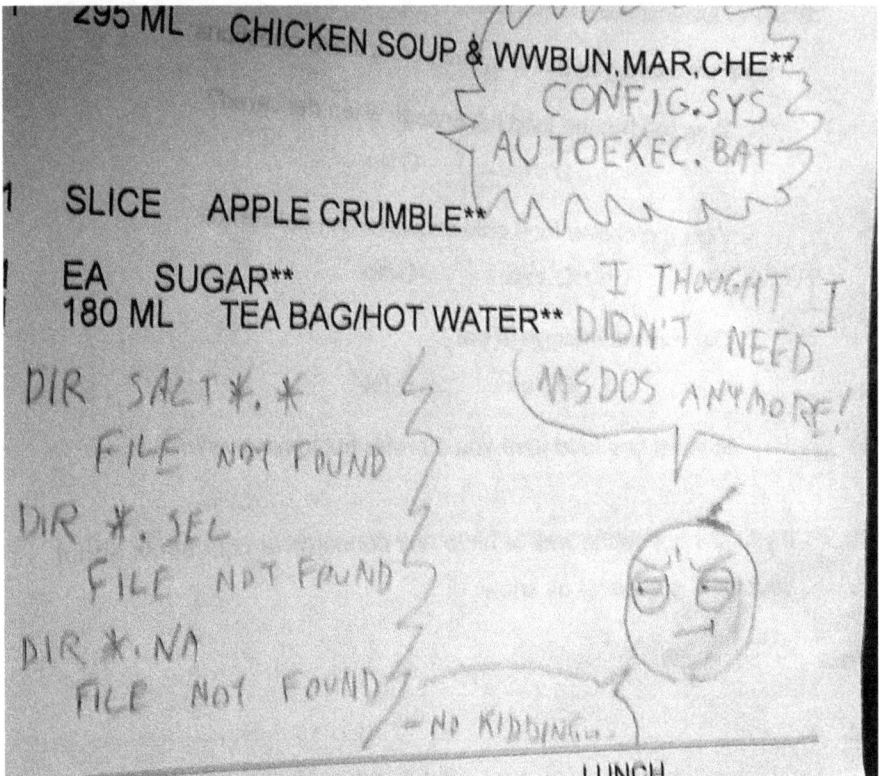

295 ML CHICKEN SOUP & WWBUN,MAR,CHE**

CONFIG.SYS
AUTOEXEC.BAT

1 SLICE APPLE CRUMBLE**

EA SUGAR**
180 ML TEA BAG/HOT WATER**

I THOUGHT I DIDN'T NEED MSDOS ANYMORE!

DIR SALT*.*
FILE NOT FOUND

DIR *.SEL
FILE NOT FOUND

DIR *.NA
FILE NOT FOUND

— NO KIDDING...

LUNCH

OK, mini DOS lesson.. (cuz the best jokes are the ones you have to explain at length... not...)

Way back before windows and macs, you had to to everything in TEXT MODE. Instead of opening a folder, you had to type in something like
"CD WHATEVER" (CD standing for 'change directory') into a prompt on an otherwise black screen such as "C:\"
Then your prompt would change to C:\WHATEVER\
If you wanted to see what files were in that folder, AHEM... directory, you might type DIR. That would spew out a list of everything in that directory. If there was a lot there, the text would zip up filling the screen and beyond, making a portion of your query's answer unreadable... so you would narrow it down.
DIR *.SEL, would show you only the files that ended with the extension SEL. DIR SALT*.* would show you all files whose name started with SALT.
AUTOEXAC.BAT and CONFIG.SYS were pretty darn essential files that basically every machine had.
And now you know everything there is to know about DOS.

So. Joke explained. Laugh now.

EA   MANDARIN ORANGE& FORTUNE CKE**

EA   SUGAR**
180 ML   TEA BAG/HOT WATER**

FORTUNE CAKE?
FORTUNE CAKE?
FORTUNE CAKE!
FORT.....   OH,

WELL, COOKIES ARE
COOL, I GUESS...

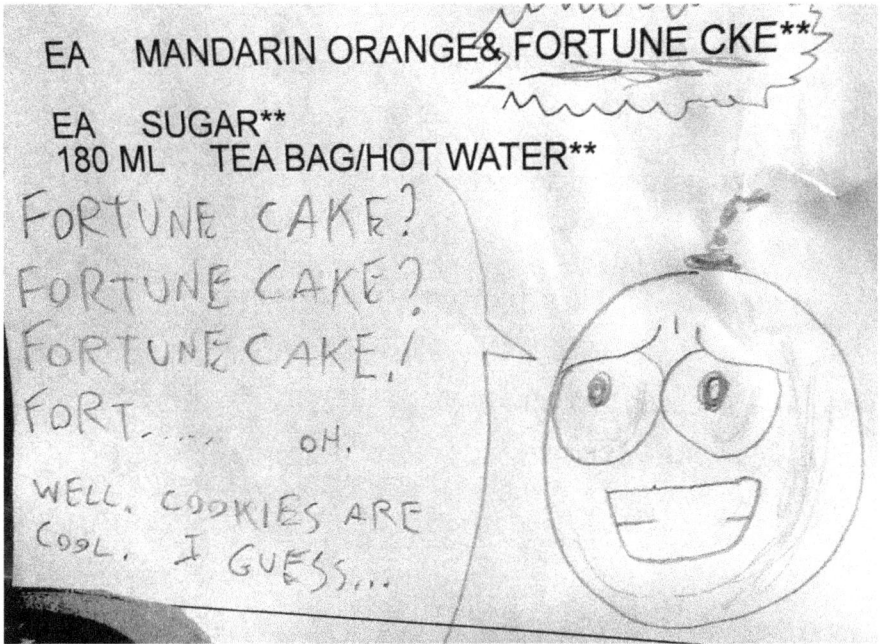

This was a new addition to the menu since 2 years ago, the fortune cookie. This shows up every few weeks alongside something like what they call a 'stir fry'.

The stir fry was a lil pile of cooked beef bits in sauce. Next to that was a separately listed pile of veggies listed as.. oh what was it... Sunrise Vegetable mix? And next to that was a lump of rice. Excuse me, rice pilaf.

What makes it a SUNRISE vegetable mix? All the colours of the sunrise... yellow from.. what is that, turnip? Orange from carrots, green from green b.. THE SUN HAS GREEN IN IT???

Okay, okay, if you're looking at a sunrise, you're probably also looking at the horizon, which could involve some nature with green grass, or trees... or Look, kitchen, I'm making excuses for you. The least you could do is send up some vodka. Jus' sayin'.

Also... a stir fry... is generally stirred. WHAAAATEVER. Stir fry by IKEA.

Oh, and the fortunes in these cookies are blander than the food. In bed.

Seriously, someone needs to start making surrealist fortune cookies. "Confucius say 'The wind on Neptune's dishwasher begs for walrus dancers in tuxedos and heavy-duty combat mecha.'" It would spark more interesting after-dinner conversation that generic inspirational platitudes.

Haiku about
penguins in greased latex
beat Confucius

EA   OATMEAL RAISIN COOKIE**

EA   SUGAR**
180 ML   TEA BAG/HOT WATER**

COOKIE HAS MANY RAISINS, YET EXPRESSED
AS ONE. MANY RAISIN. I AM ONE GRAPE,
EXPRESSED AS MANY, THE ONE GRAPES.
WHAT DOES IT MEAN? WHEN I GET
OLD AND WRINKLE, WILL I BECOME MANY,
EXPRESSED AS ONE? THE MANY GRAPE?
IS OATMEAL MY DESTINY? I'D RATHER BE WINE.

ACTR B   LUNCH

Would Tog be heartened or horrified by those dancing and singing claymation 'California Raisins'? They have limbs. Tog here doesn't. How fair is that?

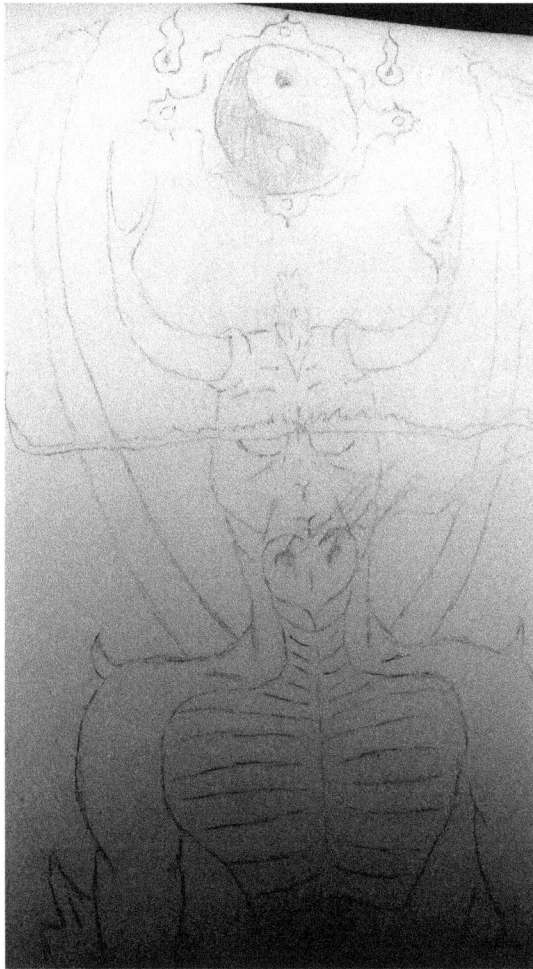

Okay, this was near the beginning of when the kids started making drawing demands of me. It started when I drew a Ninja Turtle, just to get the drawing-juices flowing, and decided to put a Minecraft pickaxe in his hand, thinking my son would get a kick out of it. He liked it, wanted me to cut it out of my HARDCOVER sketchbook. And my daughter wanted to know where hers was. So "Okay, what do you want me to draw?" I asked.

She wanted a dragon in a silly situation, so by her next visit to the hospital, I had a pic of a cartoony dragon trying to cope with living in a game of The Sims. Drawing that put me in the mood to try a SERIOUS dragon...

Started with a lil eastern appropriation, and just threw in details as I went along.

And I ended up with this. This... dopey-looking stoned cousin of Satan.

Moving on....

I sure abuse salads a lot in these things. They put such a potentially abusive verb like TOSS by it, and you're asking for trouble.

But who's heard of a HUG salad?

;TAID MILK**
E JUICE**

OTHER THAN TEA
FOR SOME REASON,
WHY DO WE END**
EACH LINE WITH **

RISPIES**

E CHEDDAR CHEESE** A PAIR OF**

ERRY BRAN MUFFIN** ASTERISKS?**

RINE**

ASTRIX?**
ASTERISKSES? **
ASTER AE?**
ASTERII?**

*

A BAG/HOT WATER

**

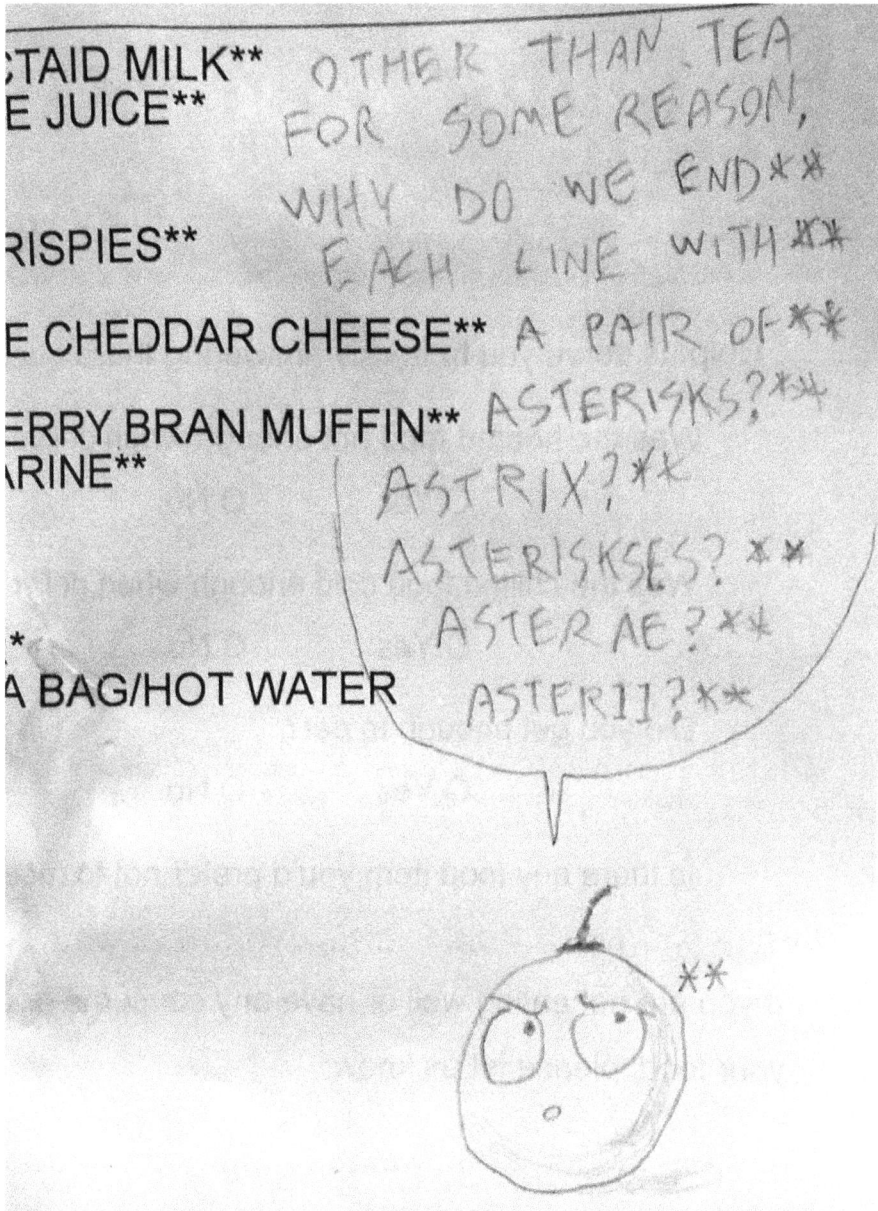

Honestly, I think this relates to the software they use, and ancient code leftovers from DOS ancestors. I'd bet you'd have to go pretty high up, and maybe ever back in time to find someone who fully grasps why they're there, and why no one's bothered to clean up the printouts to exclude them.*

*No joke about that here. Sorry. Um.. how about something about a 'DaVinci Code' style treasure?**

**No. Don't investigate that any further if you know what's good for you.

Yeah. After doing a pile of these doodles, I felt bad that the first one I made fun of only had a logo thing I drew. There. Was it worth it? Not really.

SBREADED PERCH & LEMON WEDGE**

ML   CALIFORNIA MIXED VEGETABLE**
      RED POTATO WEDGES**

E   TRIPLEBERRY CRUMBLE**

  SUGAR**
ML   TEA BAG/HOT WATER**

DINNER

    Look, I can cook, I know that's not how you BREAD something, but this makes for a clearer image than a bird perch with a lumpy coating. I guess this drawing more accurately depicts an inbread perch.

A ~~DRY MULTIGRAIN TOAST**~~
A ~~GRAPE JELLY**~~
A ~~MARGARINE**~~

A   SUGAR**
80 ML   TEA BAG/HOT WATER

Talking food items are all fun and games until you consider their fates. And grape jelly? YEESH. If you took humans, mashed them up into a paste unrecognizable from the original form and stuck a congealed portion into a little plastic container, and it enjoyed the same anthropomorphic abilities as the other foods in this book, HOW WOULD YOU REACT!? PITCHFORKS AND TORCHES!

PITCHFORKS AND TORCHES!!!

180 ML   TEA BAG/HOT WATER**

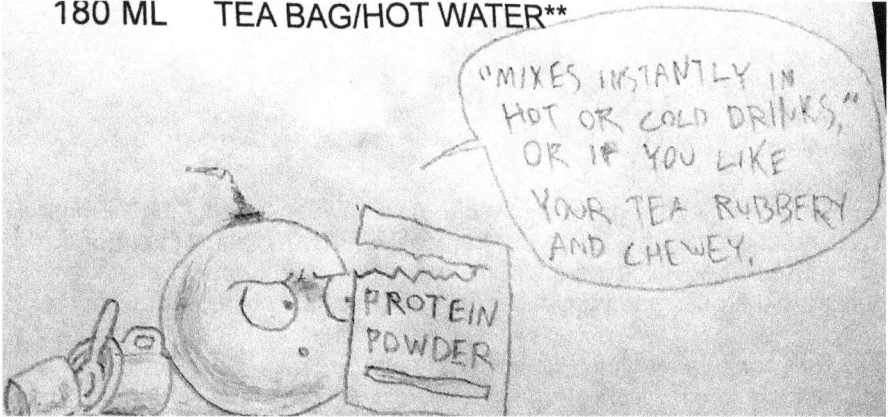

"MIXES INSTANTLY IN HOT OR COLD DRINKS," OR IF YOU LIKE YOUR TEA RUBBERY AND CHEWEY,

PROTEIN POWDER

Okay. Protein. Dandy as building materials to rebuild fleshy flesh like the wound that put me in the hospital. Since my last stay, I'd been having a lot of protein powder shakes at home.

The stuff they have in the hospital... is not the same stuff. I tried it in every consumable liquid I could get my hands on, (WHERE'S MY VODKA, PEOPLE???) and it was always horrid. I had given up, and was eating it dry right from the packet, just to get it over with.

Then apparently, the right person saw this doodle, and got me onto an alternative non-dairy milkshakey thing with protein already in it. The same stuff I'd been getting here two years ago. ... more on *that* later...

City of Fictionville
City Works and Sanitation

March 15th, 2017
Re: Insect disturbances

Dear residents,

Please do not dispose of expired protein powder, weight gain, or muscle mass products in with your normal compost. This is the time of year when many insects begin coming out from hibernation, and many of you have noticed in the past that maggots and flies often infest outdoor compost bins.

This is not generally a significant problem.

Expired protein has become a significant problem. I didn't even know that stuff would expire. Don't you muscle-types stock this for survivalist purposes or something?
Maggots and flies eat almost anything food-like, and I guess your powder counts.
Unusually muscular flies have been seen in many areas of the city. They are scaring people's pets. And that snake outbreak? Those are maggots.

Flies reproduce quickly, and if they keep getting mad gains, our city will have increasing difficulty keeping citizens safe, so please, do not dispose of protein in your compost.

Thank you,
Hugh Sorte,
Director of Sanitation

```
2    EA    WW TUNA SANDWICH**

1    125 ML   DICED PEACHES**

1    EA    SUGAR**
1    180 ML   TEA BAG/HOT WATER**
```

DID I TELL YA ABOUT MY TIME IN WORLD WAR TUNA SANDWICH? SOME PEOPLE GOT GREEN ONIONS INVOLVED. SOME? PICKLES. THAT ANGRIED UP A LOT OF FOLKS. MERCURY WEAPONS WERE BANNED, BUT THEY USED 'EM ANYWAY. THEN THE DOLPHINS GOT INVOLVED, AND THINGS GOT REALLLLY STRANGE. WWTS, I'LL NEVER FORGET.

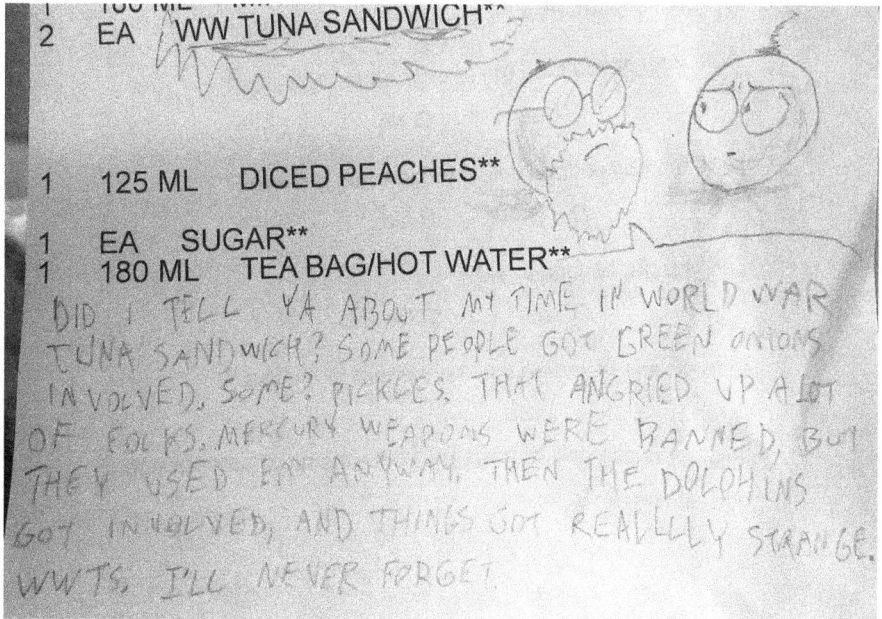

Shortly after my first stay, and I was assembling The One Grapes, I realized I missed the opportunity to use whole wheat's "WW" as "World War". So here we are at World War Tuna Sandwich.

If they make a movie based on it, it will hopefully be a more faithful adaption than WWZ.

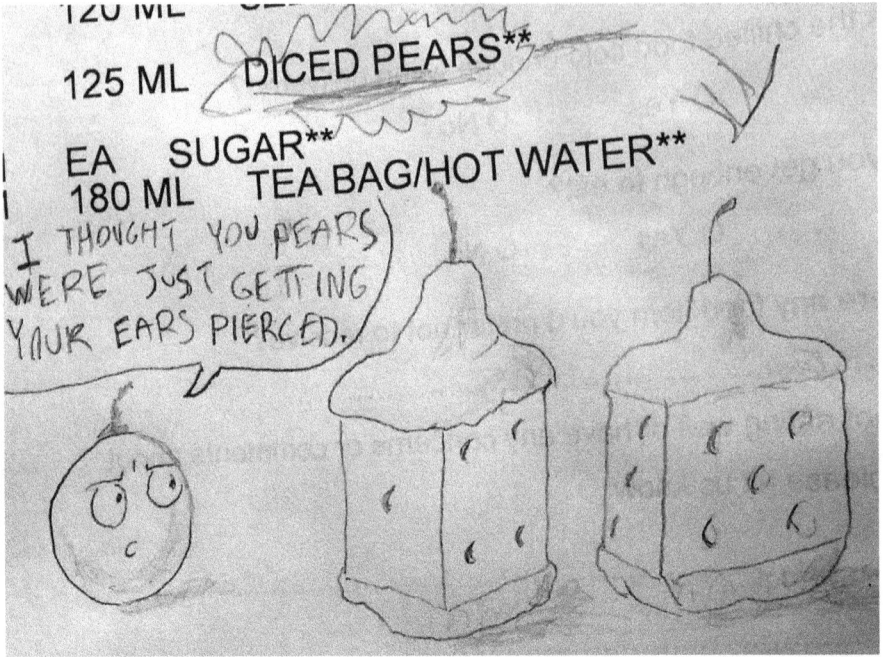

To paraphrase a conversation from Archer (the spy cartoon archer, not the archery superhero,)

"And I can't dice things into the perfect little pieces the size of.......!"
"Did you just realize why they call that kind of cutting 'dicing'?"
"...... no. I ... I knew that!"

Well frig, I had to learn it from a cartoon, *I* didn't know!

```
1   EA   APPLE SPICE BRAN MUFFIN**
1   EA   MARGARINE**


1   EA      SUGAR**
1   180 ML  TEA BAG/HOT WATER
```

HE WHO CONTROLS THE SPICE, CONTROLS THE BRAN MUFFIN!!!

For all the debate on whether the old DUNE movie was faithful to the books, or if mere mortals can withstand the slow pacing of darn near every movie of that era, (OMG, exposition! HOW LONG staring at a closeup of a character telling you things in near-monotone can we stand? She's pretty and all, but ... GET ON WITH IT!) ...

Ahem... it was a pretty neat movie, putting some awesome tropes into the general public. Stay tuned for more Dune references later. My apologies to the under-nerded people who have no idea what Dune is. Go rent the movie. But bring vodka, it's long. And slow paced, as I mentioned.

Heck, one of the fighting styles in that universe RELIES on being slow. I'm not talking *'Matrix bullet-time'* either.

It's... it's a slow movie. If you can get your hands on them, there's a miniseries of dune that's much more recent, a tad faster paced, and many even say more faithful to the books.

Screw it, rent Tremors instead. Much smaller worms, but faster paced. Bring the Vodka anyway. Kevin Bacon would want it that way. I assume.

EA   CHICKEN SANDWICH WW**

125 ML   APPLE SLICES**

EA   SUGAR**
180 ML   TEA BAG/HOT WATER**

CHICKEN SANDWICH!
WONDER WOMAN
I HEAR THERE'S A MOVIE COMING...

Huh. WW again, but not at the start. Who wants World War Chicken Sandwich so soon after World War Tuna Sandwich, anyway?

A live chicken slapped in between 2 big pieces of bread, somehow, is not as attractive as wusserface Godot. I mean Gadot. Gal Gadot.

Feels like I've been waiting forever for a Wonder Woman movie starring Godot.

COLESLAW**

'HITE SEASONED FISH**

BROCCOLI**
RICE PILAF**

APPLE CRUMBLE**

;UGAR**
    TEA BAG/HOT WATER**

MY DAUGHTER'S SUGGESTION

COLE'S LAW

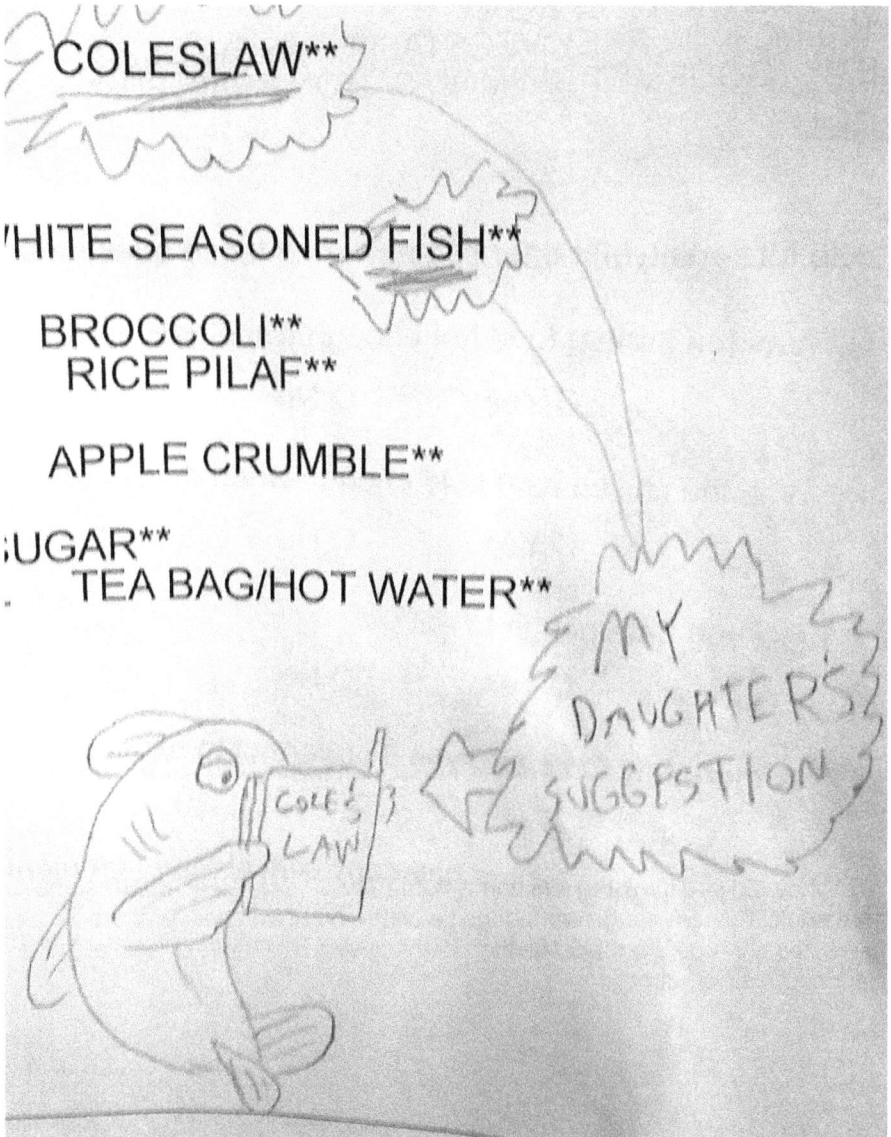

Yup. As it says, my daughter again had a notion of what I should draw. Who am I so argue? Is this a fish studying law? Is Cole a physicist? Is it a novel he's reading? Sounds like a Grisham book. My daughter didn't have the answers.

CRACKER PKG
180 ML   TURKEY VEGETABLE PASTA SOUP**
EA   GOURMET SALMON SAL ON GRAIN BUN**

"TURKEY-VEGETABLE"
GARDEN

125 ML   DICED PEACHES**

What, did you think turkeys came from EGGS? Silly, CHICKENS come from eggs. Turkeys are grown alongside all the other veggies, and are harvested soon before thanksgiving. Thanksgiving is a harvest festival, not a slaughter festival, duh!

\ BROWN SUGAR**
0 ML   CREAM OF WHEAT**
\   PEANUT BUTTER**

\   BISCUIT**
\   GRAPE JELLY**
\   MARGARINE**

\   SUGAR**
0 ML   TEA BAG/HOT WATER

YUP, I'M WORKING ON IT, BUT FIRST I GOTTA MILK THE WHEAT, DON'T I? WELL I CAN'T EVEN FIND THE UDDER!

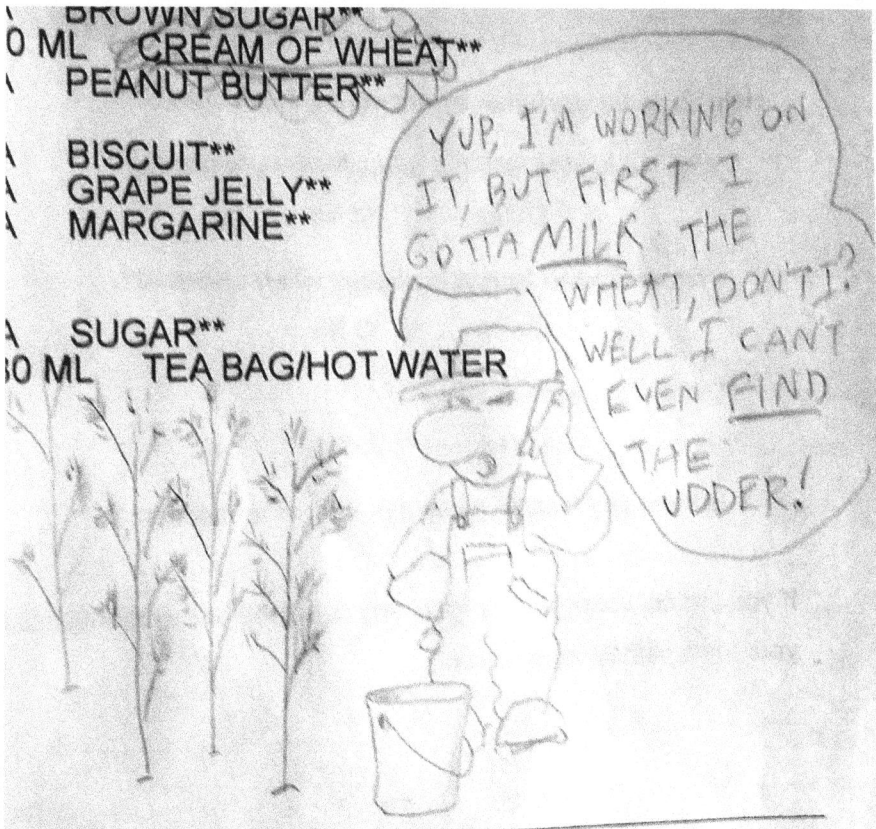

CREAM of wheat. Implying MILK of wheat. Implying someone milks the wheat. My new, unnamed farmer character sets out to supply the demand.

Should we name him? Naaaah.

So... cream of wheat. What the heck is this pasty gob that showed up on my tray? I tried it, I had heard of it, but had no preconceptions. It... came with a little packet of brown sugar. After my first attempt at eating the cream of wheat, (brown sugar helped very little), I forever after used the brown sugar in my tea.

Let's take a moment to address the little paper packets that sugar comes in here. The trays are often home to hot condensation. Worse, from time to time, one overfilled or tipsy tea or coffee can spell a bit of a spill for half the trays of the ward, when they're all arranged atop each other in the transport rack.

Little paper packets aren't fond of that either. Somehow it can suck out all the empty space in the packet, maybe by slight congealing, the sugar takes up more space, meaning there's no empty space in the packet to rip through. Kay, it's really no huge deal to rip through a thin wall of sugar. It's just... huh. I have a spent sugar packet near me right now... does the paper... No, that's stupid. I won't taste garbage. But... science... Nope. Cross-contamination with a used teabag. I can't run a lab in these conditions.

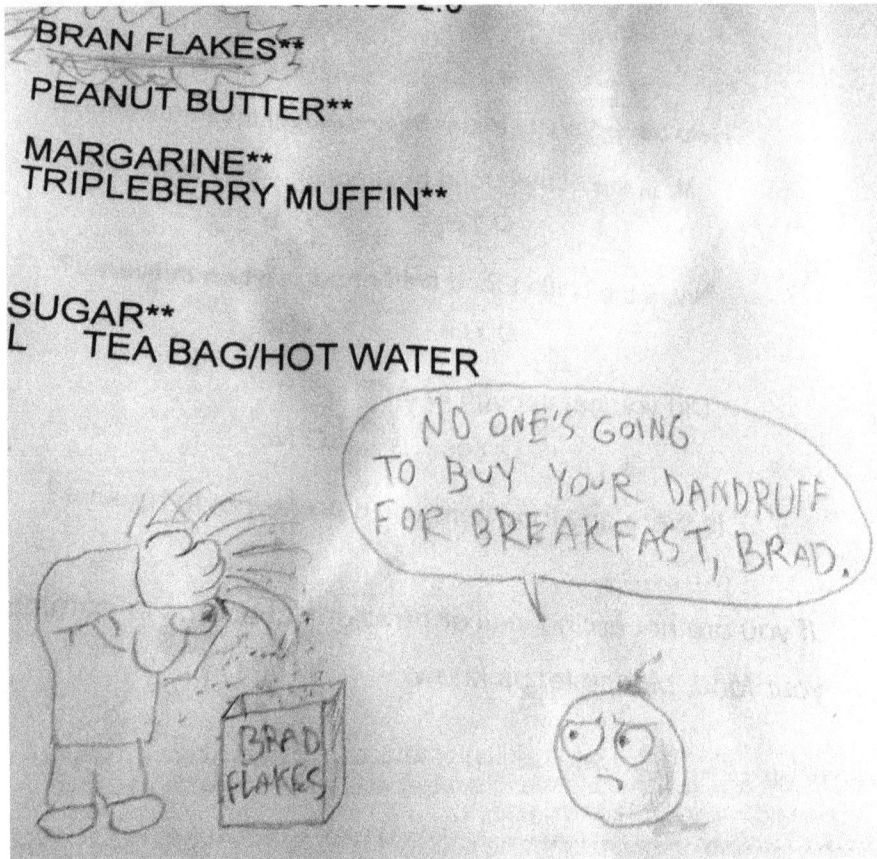

Given my lactose intolerance, and marked distaste for eggs and oatmeal, my array of breakfast options is a little narrow. A cereal is always part of my compete breakfast, be they bran flakes, corn flakes, cheerios (that are often less than crunchy for reasons I can only speculate,) or rice crispies.

Yes, I listen to the rice crispies.

No, they don't tell me anything interesting.

PARAPLEGIC VAMPIRE

I VANT TO SUCK YOUR BLOOD!!!

-BUT- YOU HAVE TO INVITE ME IN FIRST.

-AND DO YOU HAVE A RAMP?

Random art idea.

Some writers have it so that when you get turned into a vamp, your current physical condition becomes eternal. That would not be ideal for me! I'll take the health-reset style, TYVM, but it raised some questions.

Transformations would be really handy. They always seem to be able to transform into a bat or wolf, or whatever, but when they change back, they generally seem to have their clothes.
Could this vamp here also take his wheelchair into the transformation? Yay! He'd be able to shift to mist, or whatever, go inside, then turn into humanoid again. If his chair is still outside, it would be awkward.

I've seen vamps transform and their animal forms reflect what they were wearing. A bright red shirt might be represented as some red fur on the bat, or something. If this vamp sucked up the chair, would the animal have wheels? Geez, what if the animal was also a paraplegic?

Screw this, I'm holding out for the full-conversion cyborg body instead. I'M WAITING, ELON!

```
I     EA     CHOCOLATE CHIP COOKIE**

1     EA     SUGAR**
1     180 ML     TEA BAG/HOT WATER**
```

SEE? THAT'S A CHOCOLATE CHIP COOKIE. NOT CHIPS. BUT THE COOKIE THAT SHOWED UP WAS ACTUALLY A CHOCOLATE CHIPS COOKIE. PLURALS ARE HARD. I UNDERSTAND. BUT CHIPS HAVE MORE LACTOSE THAN A CHIP. ATE IT HAPPILY ANYWAY.
-THE ONE GRAPES

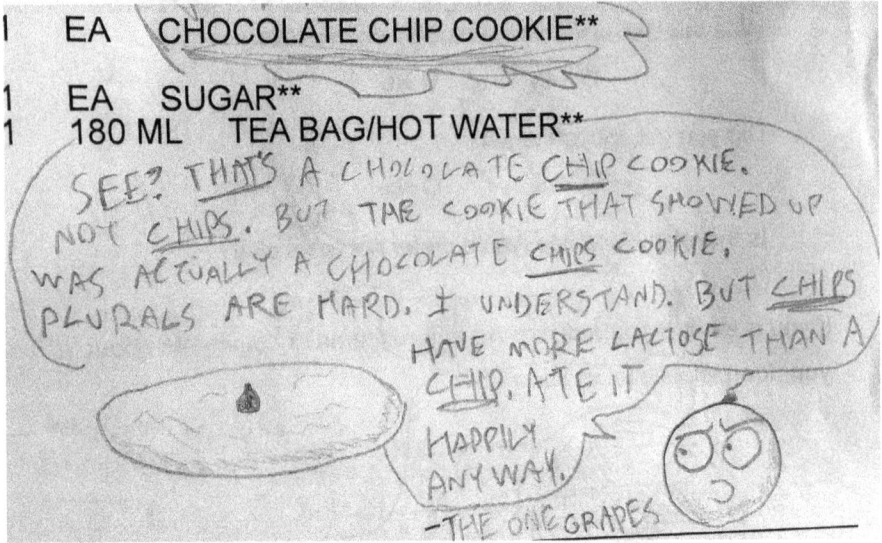

Notice how Tog is taking on an increasingly narrator-like role recently? He's cute, he's fun, but what an awful name. Tog of course, short for 'The One Grapes'.

Since this second book is The Many Grape, maybe he could change his name to Tmg. Which is unpronounceable. T'mug? Timag? TIMMAY!!!!...

No. Tog he remains. To be confused with a caveman or something.

Or Pogs.

Okay, by this time in my stay, it had been a regular thing for my kids to make art requests from me. I asked my daughter what she wanted this time, and she said "Mercy."

Which confused her mother, which made me laugh. My daughter had been sucked in to the aesthetics of the game Overwatch, and somehow managed to convince momma to buy her the game. Yeah, it's violent, but not bloody, and the online community seems to be much politer than I'd expect. Usually it's my wife who's more restrictive on types of games, so if she was OK with it, I can't argue. I look forward to giving it a shot myself. (At the time of writing this very section, I look to have another week and a half to go in hospital... barring any mess ups like the one yesterday that came down to someone else's paperwork mess-up delaying me by a week... Long, boring story. grr.)

ANYWAY, with my minuscule net access here through my cell, I got a reference picture of Mercy. This is the kind of thing I would have drawn in my early 20s, except coloured on the computer, not a copy of an existing character, and with bigger... wings. Or y'know. Weapons.

My son, now knowing he could request video game characters, asked for his favourite character from Undertale. Suits me, Sans is awesome. This was one of the few times a general concept in my head came out onto paper very closely to match.

Background on Sans- He's friendly, and if you behave in the game, he's your buddy every time you run into him, and a fountain of bad jokes and puns.

If you behave badly, and kill kill kill... he'll warn you to shape up, or you're going to have... a bad time. If you continue down the dark side, he'll attack you as the 'final' boss. And he is hard as heck. And has an amazing retro soundtrack to his fight. To top it off, he's kind of aware of the fact that he's in a video game, and remembers your actions from former playthroughs... so I can imagine him being very torn if you were the hero in your first playthrough, then a villain he needs to kill next time- hence his teariness in this pic above.

Shut up, skeletons can cry.

Half his attacks involve those skulls that appear for a split second before unleashing huge lasers. Because obviously. My daughter would no doubt wish me to inform you that they are called "Gaster Blasters", which ... has a whole story onto itself.

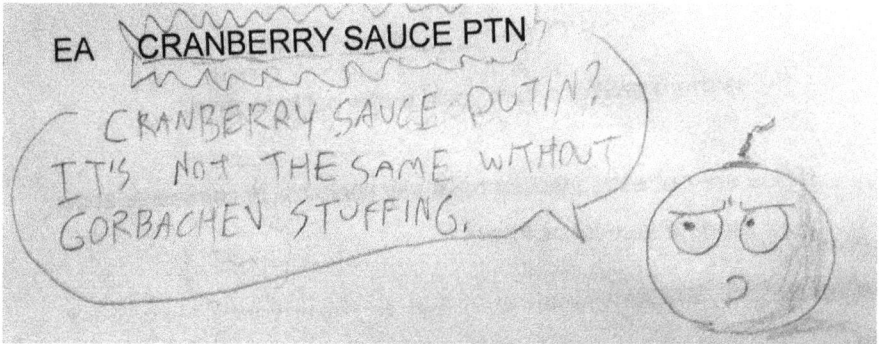

EA CRANBERRY SAUCE PTN

CRANBERRY SAUCE PUTIN? IT'S NOT THE SAME WITHOUT GORBACHEV STUFFING.

Who misses Gorby? Who remembers Gorby?

I could have made a joke for *Cranberry Sauce POUTINE*... but that might actually be a good idea. Sounds yummy. Maybe.

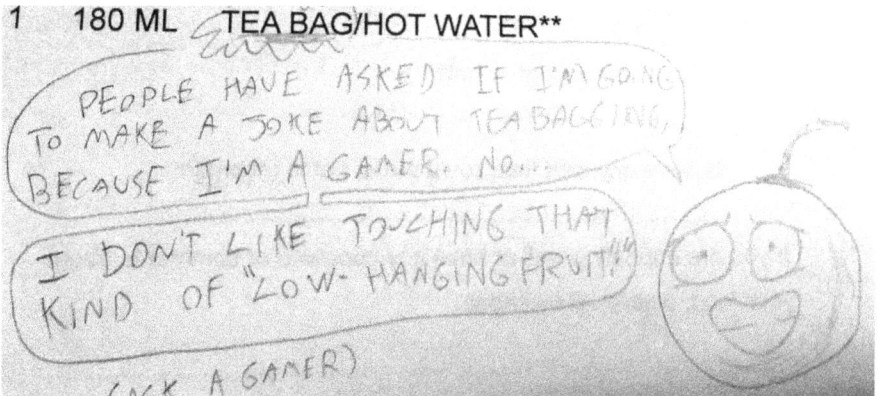

1   180 ML   TEA BAG/HOT WATER**

PEOPLE HAVE ASKED IF I'M GOING TO MAKE A JOKE ABOUT TEA BAGGING, BECAUSE I'M A GAMER. NO...

I DON'T LIKE TOUCHING THAT KIND OF "LOW-HANGING FRUIT!"

(ncK A GAMER)

I'm aware 'teabagging' wasn't invented by video gamers, but dang if they didn't popularize it. What dolt came up with it in the first place? Seems like a big bite-risk.

ow.

6 EA ASIAN STYLE MEATBALLS**
120 ML RICE**
120 ML SZECHWAN BLEND VEGETABLE**

EA MANDARIN ORANGE& FORTUNE CKE**

EA SUGAR**
180 ML TEA BAG/HOT WATER**

ASIAN STYLE MEATBALLS? SO DOES THAT MEAN SWEET & SOUR? OMG. YOU'RE JUST THAT S&S MEATBALL FROM TWO YEARS AGO, AREN'T YOU???

I KNOW NUSSING!!

DINNER

Not being a time traveller, I can't compare side by side, but I'm pretty sure it's the same dish, renamed. If I end up in the hospital again (let's face it, eventually...) it better not be named Brazilian meatballs.

Nameless farmer returns, faced again with milking the unmilkable. I'd been so aware of the pills, I forgot they made lactose-free milk. Too bad it's pricier.

1 SLICE BANANA CAKE**
1 EA SUGAR**
1 180 ML TEA BAG/HOT WATER**

WOW, A CAKE FOR ME?

YEAH, I FIGURED I'D DO SOMETHING NICE, SINCE I SAW "HALF BANANA" ON THE LUNCH MENU TOMORROW.

WHA... WHAT??

I MEANT "HAPPY BIRTHDAY!!!"

I'll say one thing for the hospital food, there's some really nice desserts. Worth a bit of lactose. The banana cake was nice, but the brownies? Dark chocolate (lower in lactose than milk chocolate, obviously, and I prefer it anyway...) with big chunks of chocolate hiding in the cakey part. That one shows up every other week or so... More please!

Deserts and soups... I'll be honest, they've been pretty darn reliably good in here.

2 EA · 180 ML · MINESTRONE SOUP**
ASIAN NOODLE & CHICKEN SALAD**

ALL THE YEARS I WASTED ON THAT GLOWING FRISBEE, WHEN I COULD HAVE BEEN THROWING MINES AT PEOPLE!

1 · 125 ML · TROPICAL FRUIT SALAD**

1 · EA · SUGAR**
1 · 180 ML · TEA BAG/HOT WATER**

THAT'S... GOOD?

MINES-TRON

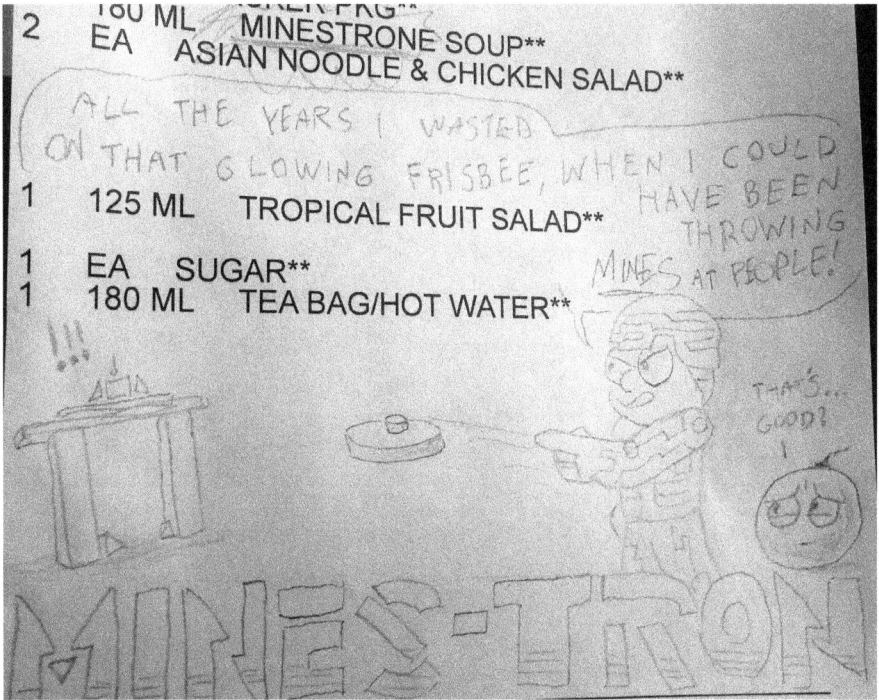

Speaking of soups...! Thankfully my lactose ban spares me from 'cream of' anything... cream of mushroom, cream of clam... I'm no fan of mushrooms or shellfish as it is, much less in thick sludge.

Oh, and that asian noodle & chicken salad up top? If they'd served the chicken part warm, and ditched the sad salad and noodles, it could be really good. They do OK little salads in general... this one... is an exception. Other than the chicken. Which needs to be warmed. Meh.

2	EA	WW SALMON SANDWICH**
1	SLICE	TRIPLEBERRY CRUMBLE**
1	EA	SUGAR**
1	180 ML	TEA BAG/HOT WATER**

ANOTHER REDACTED DOCUMENT? LETS SEE....
SO, THE ILLUMINATI TOOK MY MASHED POTATO- AGAIN. IT'S OBVIOUS NOW- THEY DON'T WANT ME BUILDING ANY MORE ALIEN LANDING PADS!!!

IF THEY THINK I CAN'T BUILD ONE FROM SALMON SALAD, THEY HAVE ANOTHER THING COMING! SOMETHING GLOWING AND SPINNY, WITH GREY-SKINNED DUBSTEP DJs IN IT. OH! YOU DIDN'T KNOW THAT DUBSTEP WAS FIRST BROUGHT TO EARTH IN THE 80's BY THE GREYS? THATS WHY THEY CALL YOU SHEEP!

LACTR, R WAKE UP BEFORE THE GREYS DROP THE BASS!!!

LUNCH
SATURDAY
18/03/2017
RM00515959

Tolja mashed potatoes would come up again. And now you know all about another dimension, new galaxy; intergalactic, planetary.

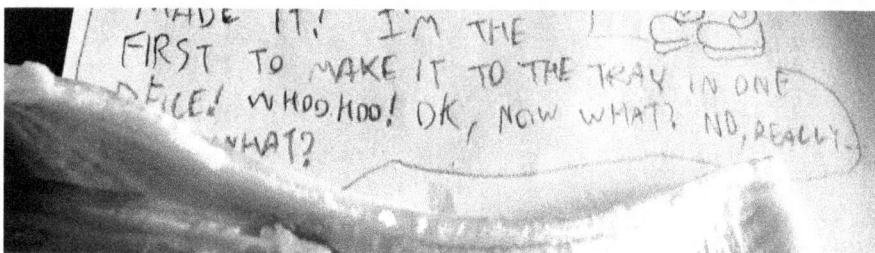

Congratulations, Banana. You've won Running man. Enjoy your tropical retirement of riches. – As I skin you and devour your innards, concealing your fate to all future runners.

Mua.

Muaha.

MuAHAHAHAHAHAHHAHAHAHAHHAAHAHAAAAA!!!!!!!!!!

So, this was what replaced that horrid tiny packet of protein. Lactose free 'milkshake' thing, vanilla flavour. Not amazing, but not terrible. I've cropped out the brand and company I'm supposed to be boycotting. Last time I had anything from them was this product, two years ago. Their big sin is water-rights related, but when I look closer at this, I see another glaring issue...

Okay, so "2.0 cal/ml." Okay. Fine. 2.0. That point-zero implies a regulated, exacting number. BUT, they slipped up, right below on the front of the box. "477 Cal per 237 ml serving". Basic math... 237 ml at 2.0 cal *should* equal 474 cal.

They're slipping in an extra three calories in every box! OBVIOUSLY they're trying to fatten people up! Three calories multiplied by however many of these boxes get consumed daily? Forget fast foods and soda! This will fatten us all up in preparation for our alien overlords' harvest!

Let's ignore that I drink these for the protein, and none of the calories are needed at all. Let's also ignore the bottle of cola sitting next to me as I type this.

.... it SHOULD say 2.012658227848101 cal / ml. Sheesh.

City of Fictionville
City Works and Sanitation

April 11th, 2017
Re: Alligators

Dear residents,

Firstly, thank you, as most of you have stopped disposing of expired protein products via compost. Unfortunately, the size of the flies has not notably decreased. They seem to have found other sources of protein.

Secondly, we've noticed a significant decrease in common rodent populations.
And birds. No one misses rats, but even the crows have a welcome place in our city.

Thirdly, it seems in lieu of using the compost bins, many of you have been flushing expired protein down your toilets. It has a chance of clogging pipes, but this is a much lesser concern over the effects on certain urban wildlife that unfortunately has been making their home in lower sewer areas.
This seems to be a refuge for the rats, but also- remember the urban myth about flushed baby alligators? There's been some revelations to that notion.
Gators with sick pecs and biceps have been spotted near the river, flexing and smiling at women. I'm not trained for this, and the city will have difficulty raising money to deal with these gators safely.
In the meantime, please dispose of for protein products in the regular garbage, or, I don't know, fireplaces? And stay away from the river.
We don't think the muscular gators are any faster than normal gators, as they only seem to be working the front legs and chest. I discovered that on top of usual zig-zag running, dropping your sunglasses distracts them until they can put them on, after which, they seem to feel the need to pose for each other for a while.

Thank you,
Hugh Sorte,
Director of Sanitation

180 ML   VEGETABLE SOUP
         NAVY BEAN CURRY & KALE**

120 ML   RICE

125 ML   DICED PEACHES**

EA   SUGAR**
180 ML   TEA BAG/HOT WATER**

Seriously. Navy bean? What? The dish itself was a mix of … stuff... a few of the object types in it may have been the bean in question, but I have no idea. More surprising. it was GOOD. Like, "how did this get into the hospital" good? One of the rare dishes with any kind of spicy kick. This was *not* around 2 years ago.

Sign me up for more of these and a lot less of … "chicken thigh & gravy." ....so fatty...... a lot of otherwise fine sounding foods are tarnished by fat. Many with just an edge, easily ignored, but not that chicken thigh. The gravy is no help either. Pale and tasteless, it serves only as camouflage to make it harder to cut off the chunks of fat from the chicken. In the first week, I considered that dish an ally, but I got to know it better...

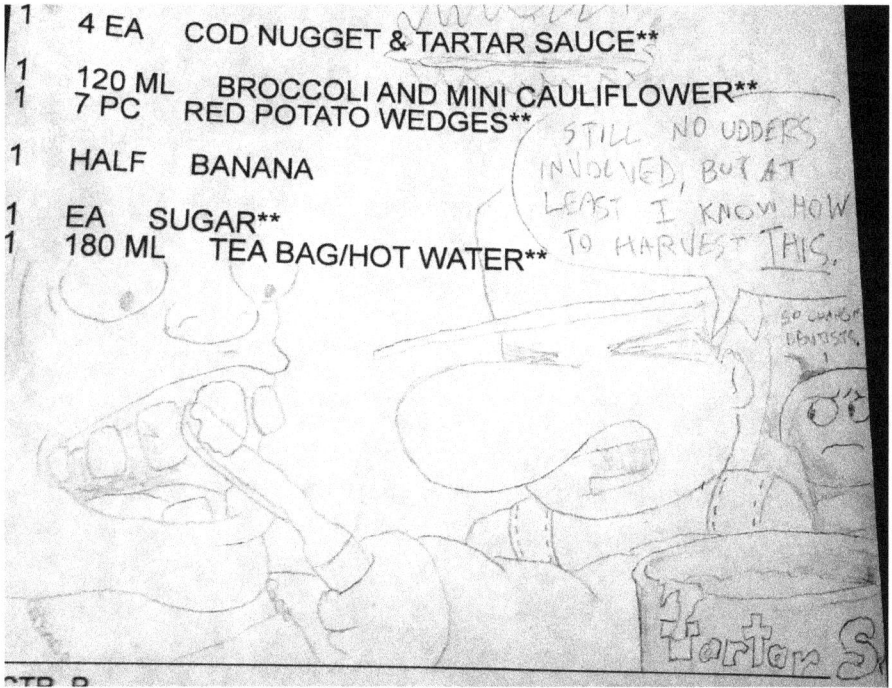

Okay, nameless farmer is back. Tartar was a word that I thought for years I was mishearing in either the context of sauce, or teeth. Or that it was some kind of gag that adults had between themselves that just didn't seem that funny to kids.

Now I'm 40. Is it funny yet? Clearly, it Is not.

My apologies.

2   180 ML   BEEF STEW & WW BUN & MARG**

1   SLICE   APPLE CRUMBLE**

1   EA   SUGAR**
1   180 ML   TEA BAG/HOT WATER**

Wild West
Bun &
Marge

Here's a couple ideas I'm actually surprised I didn't use two years ago.

That bun... does he look like he has a butt for a face? The actual bun had a dent/fold a lot like that, but no, now it's a buttface.

And does his hat remind you of anything? A certain cheesy cowboy in commercials from ages past?

Notice how cheese sometimes just advertises CHEESE in general, not a specific brand? Hmm.... another illuminati plot to fatten us up for the impending alien overlords.

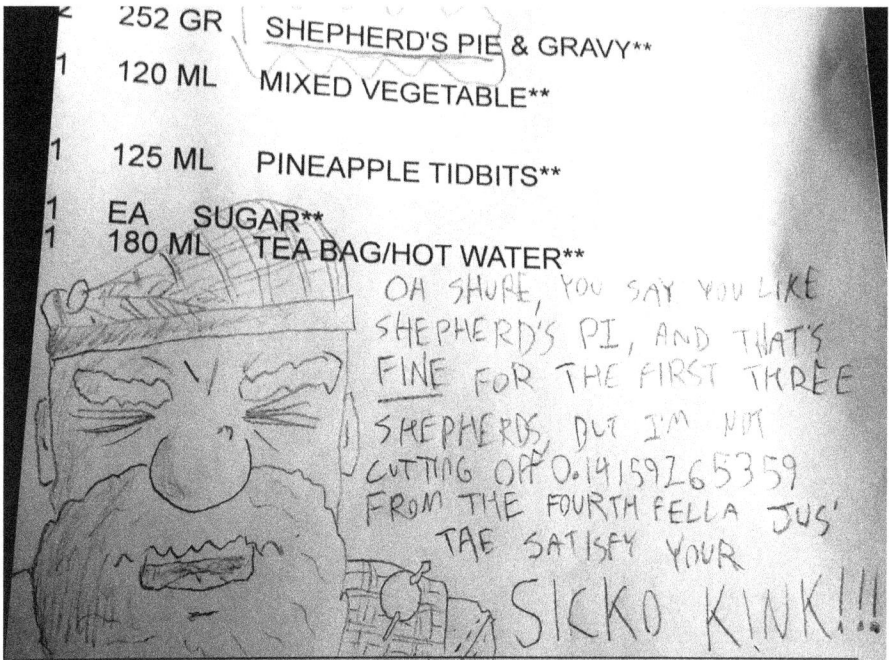

```
2   252 GR    SHEPHERD'S PIE & GRAVY**
1   120 ML    MIXED VEGETABLE**

1   125 ML    PINEAPPLE TIDBITS**

1   EA    SUGAR**
1   180 ML    TEA BAG/HOT WATER**
```

OH SHURE, YOU SAY YOU LIKE SHEPHERD'S PI, AND THAT'S FINE FOR THE FIRST THREE SHEPHERDS, BUT I'M NOT CUTTING OFF 0.14159265359 FROM THE FOURTH FELLA JUS' TAE SATISFY YOUR SICKO KINK!!!

Alternatively, I could have drawn a sliced up shepherd, or had a shepherd worrying WHERE this 0.14159265359 portion would be cut from. That could have gotten ugly really quickly, so instead, I'll just leave your imagination to come up with something far more gorrifying.

Wow. Bet typo I've made in a long time. I'm leaving it. Gorrifying. That's it, I hereby instate my authority as a hack writer to declare that to be a REAL WORD. Excuse me, I have to go tell the internet. Hold please...

There. And here's proof. I declared it here, and to the internet in a thread about writers creating words.. It's official. Gorrifying. Use it, and think of grapes.

Joseph Picard
I just typoed one into existence.
Gorrifying.
I declared it a word, and am notifying the readers as such. Y'all can use it. Gorrifying. Like horrifying but messier.

I'm sure no one else ever came up with that ever ever.

Just now · Like · Reply · More

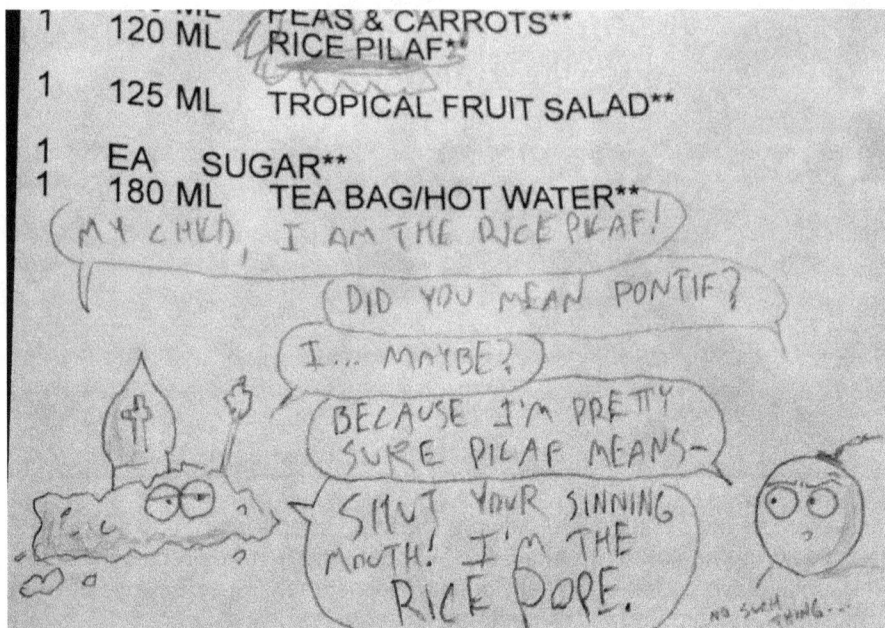

Please read with a heavy Italian accent in your head. Awwwww, I should have written it like that. I'ma de rice-a-pilafa!... maybe not.

I'll save that for my Mario impressions.

Did I ever tell ya about how my wife's aunt always made salmon fillet whenever I happened to be going over for dinner, then word got to her that I wasn't big on fish, but she heard this only *after* I'd come to *like* salmon due to her cooking, but in consideration to me, she made something else just as I was looking forward to her salmon?

Did I ever tell you I can write run-on sentences? Yeah, that's just a bite. A writer learns to not do that kind of thing, but that also trains us how to *use* that dark power. Have you heard of a wall-o-text? I've seen walls that would make Trump blush.

I've seen things. Things you people won't believe. Walls of text on fire off the shoulder of Orion. I watched run on sentences glitter in the dark near the Tannhauser Gate. All that grammar will be lost in time... like forum posts in rain. Time to edit.

Okay, I just really want to watch Bladerunner today, okay?

Oh, and salmon salad sandwiches? They do not share my favour with my wife's aunt's salmon fillet. In case you couldn't guess.

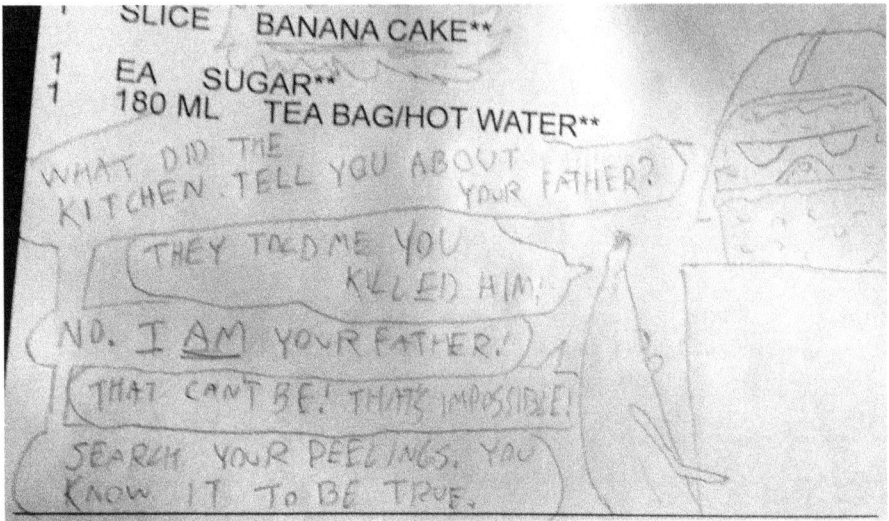

SLICE BANANA CAKE**
1 EA SUGAR**
1 180 ML TEA BAG/HOT WATER**

WHAT DID THE KITCHEN TELL YOU ABOUT YOUR FATHER?

THEY TOLD ME YOU KILLED HIM!

NO. I AM YOUR FATHER!

THAT CAN'T BE! THAT'S IMPOSSIBLE!

SEARCH YOUR PEELINGS. YOU KNOW IT TO BE TRUE.

So, when I came up with this idea, I didn't know if all that text would fit on the little slip of paper. I mused out loud while a kitchen staffer was grabbing the tray that I might have to draw the concept out on a full page. Her eyes lit up. WELL. Despite being able to fit it on the regular slip after all, I felt like I had an expectation to meet..... so...

180 ML CHICKEN STEW & WW BUN & MARG**

120 ML CORN**

125 ML PINEAPPLE TIDBITS**

EA SUGAR**
180 ML TEA BAG/HOT WATER**

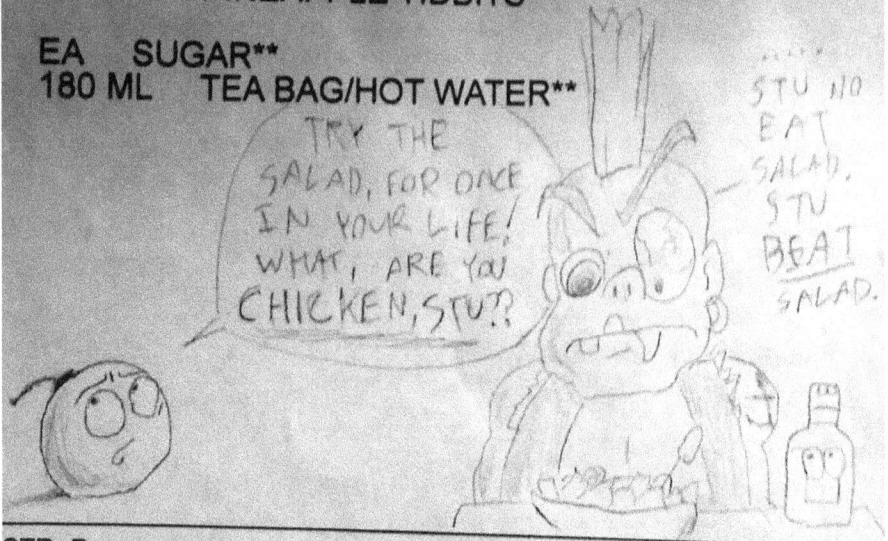

TRY THE SALAD, FOR ONCE IN YOUR LIFE! WHAT, ARE YOU CHICKEN, STU?

STU NO EAT SALAD. STU BEAT SALAD.

I hadn't been drawing many of these for a while, and a kitchen staffer gave me a bit of a hard time about it. She said she even had an idea for me for dinner's selection.

She told me what dinner was going to be when she grabbed the lunch tray! I had a sneak preview! Chicken stew!

Yeah, don't laugh, it's one of the better things that show up. As per typical, BLAND. But really good within that parameter.

Oh by the way, as of this drawing, this recurring punk guy now officially has a name. Yay, Stu! It's your naming day! You're going to make Pog jealous with a name like that. I mean Tog. Whatever.

1   EA   HOT CROSS BUN
1   EA   MARGARINE**

EA   SUGAR**
180 ML   TEA BAG/HOT WATER

I PLAYED THAT BLASTED TUNE 1000 TIMES AS A KID, AND IT SUMMONS ONE BUN. MY WHOLE LIFE... AND ONE BUN.

In elementary school, I, like many, were forced to learn to play the recorder. And what song was easy to teach kids? Hot Cross Buns. I had no idea what a hot cross bun was, or what significance it had. I gathered from context that it was... a bun. Big deal. Didn't know it had any religious roots, or that it was an Easter thing. Then this shows up one morn.

And it was very yummy. There were raisins in it. The nurse told me I'd have to wait about a year for the next one. I should have told her I wanted one for every X-box day, and as a gamer, I needed half a dozen every Monday. I'd feel guilty though, I'm a Playstation player.

1 EA CRACKER PKG
1 180 ML MINESTRONE SOUP**
2 EA ASIAN NOODLE & CHICKEN SALAD**

1 125 ML TROPICAL FRUIT SALAD**

1 EA SUGAR**
1 180 ML TEA BAG/HOT WATER**

WHAT'S WRONG, CHICKEN. SALAD?

THAT MAN IS THE BANE OF MY PEOPLE, AND BEING THIS CLOSE PUTS MY OWN LIFE IN GREAT PERIL. I THINK BEING AFRAID IS WARRENTED.

OH, THEN WHAT I SAID IS KIND OF IN—

YES. IT WAS.

And here's Stu again. Salad is being chicken, and justifiably so. Excuse him for being terse. Yeah, this is the same salad that would do better if the chicken were separate, hot, and the salad were... better. I get what they're trying to do here, it's a fancy idea, it just doesn't work out well in a format where the food spends time sitting around before delivery. I guess.

GF strong had this problem in spades when I was there in 2001-2002... when you got mobile enough, you were well advised to show up at the cafeteria for lunch and dinner if you could. It wasn't generally amazing food, but when it got put into transport trays, and migrated up to people's beds, the cold things were not cold, the not things were not hot, and everything was squishier than it should be. Since then, I've heard tales of improvement, and tales of worsening. As of this moment? No idea. Entirely possible they're getting food through the same suppliers at this hospital.

May Tog have mercy on our souls.

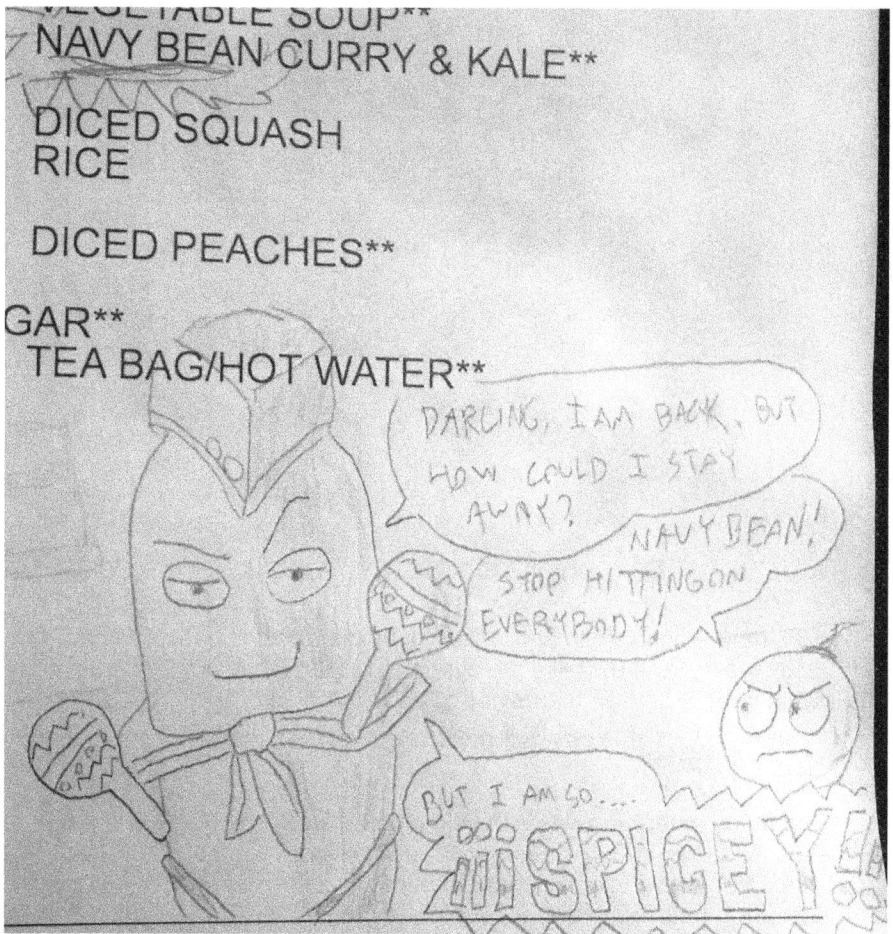

I wish this guy could be a more frequent character, but he doesn't show up on my tray much. He's yummy.

So.... 'Spicey' vs 'Spicy'. I try to write in the official Canadian spellings of things, which generally means the U.K. Way of spellings things, most notably color vs colour. Lots of U involved.

Quite often, U.S. Spellings are newer, and sometimes deliberate little snubs to the U.K., especially freshly after independence. U.K. Chose to call the last letter in the alphabet "zed". U.S. Chose "zee". And to cement it, they made an alphabet song, which handily rhymed when you say zee, but not if you use zed. – Unless you rename "v", "ved". (I'm not stopping you.)

There were tons of names for 'z' being tossed around by many people for a long time. It wasn't that popular of a letter for a time. They finally decided, and the U.S. said "YOU CAN'T MAKE US CALL IT THAT!!!"

So now you know. I'm educational.

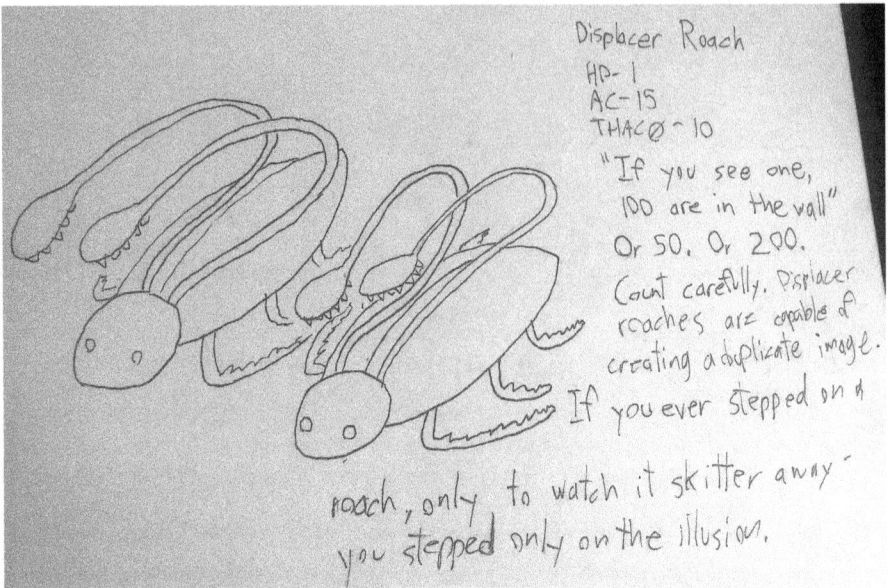

Displacer Roach
HP- 1
AC- 15
THAC0 - 10
"If you see one,
100 are in the wall"
Or 50. Or 200.
Count carefully. Displacer
roaches are capable of
creating a duplicate image.
If you ever stepped on a
roach, only to watch it skitter away -
you stepped only on the illusion.

Okay, nerd time! A while ago, I saw an article about a spider that had an outer body that looked a lot like a ladybug (a.k.a. Ladybird... not that I ever knew what a red beetle with dots had to do with ladies or birds..)

Anyway, that spider uses its appearance to help it hunt, and is called the ladybird *mimic* spider.

Now, many a nerd familiar with Dungeons & Dragons, (D&D or games that take inspiration from it) hear '*mimic*', and are reminded of a monster that looks like a treasure chest, or other tempting object. An adventurer who fails to see the truth until too late is in trouble. So I thought, if a mimic can have an insect counterpart, why not other bugs, with other D&D critters?

The displacer beast is a monster from D&D that looks a lot like a panther, with long tentacles rising from its back, each with a spiked pod. (much like I have coming off the roaches in the drawing) Its big trick is being able to create an illusion of itself to throw off enemies, who are generally unsure of which displacer beast is the real one, and which is an illusion.

The text I wrote by the drawing is supposed to partly *mimic* (ah? See what I did there??) the way monsters are presented in D&D rulebooks.

And as I mentioned much earlier, the best jokes are always the ones you need to explain.

Meh, my D&D folks got it right away.

Beeholder

Almost dead or freshly dead, as long as the stingers and venom are intact, six bees are the weapons of the Bee-holder, leaving only two legs to walk on. Often mistaken by predators for a small bee swarm attacking a spider, the Bee-holder is also known as "Nope, nope, nope, nope, #@! that $#!?, nope."

HP- YOU attack it first!
AC- no, really. Nope.
THACØ - OMG, run.

And my D&D folk will definitely know of the 'beholder', the big fleshy floating pod with one big eye in the middle, and a pile of 'eye stalks' sporting eyes with various powers. Very bad news.

Well, I thought the insect kingdom could use a version. Too bad, we got an arachnid, not an insect. OH WAIT! This arachnid has 6 insects at its disposal!

It holds bees!

It's a bee-holder!

What is more impressive, an arachnid getting the idea to use bees as weapons, the ability to effectively wield them, or the ability to walk around on one quarter on the usual number of legs.

I suppose low-level beeholders might only use one bee until it gets more adept.

Now that I think of it, D&D has rules for giant versions of pretty much any bug. I thought of the beeholder as being about the size of a real tarantula, but in the D&D world, why not the size of a VW bug, using bees the size of horse heads? Now THERE'S a threat!

Gelatinous Honey
Did you know? A Gelatinous Cube poops. Well, they leave behind a mildly acidic residue. A lucky breed of bee is immune, and even thrives upon it. Their sting is often quickly debilitating. But the honey? Sweet, tangy.— And only HALF as corrosive as universal solvent.

One last one for the D&D crew. This one's not really a joke, so much as a general idea. The classic monster "gelatinous cube" is a giant wad of jello-type material that wanders the halls of dungeons, and will bring victims into its body to dissolve/eat, leaving behind things like bones, stones, and metals, which stay trapped inside its body until someone defeats it,

I propose that the cube leaves behind *something* as some form of defecation. This idea started as the honey in a honeycomb being little gelatinous... hexahedrons... and what would people do with that?

Try to eat it.

Because... humans are dumb and experimental.

1 EA OATMEAL RAISIN COOKIE**

1 EA SUGAR**
1 180 ML TEA BAG/HOT WATER**

1 EA PEPPER
1 EA SALT

I... I know these words, but... I thought it was just a legend!

IN THE SIXTH DAY OF THE THIRD MONTH of THE GREAT VIGIL, APRIL TWENTY-THREE, WHEN THE STITCHES WERE CAST ASIDE, THE KITCHEN SAID, "LET THERE BE PEPPER" AND THERE WAS. AND THE KITCHEN SAID "LET THERE BE SALT." AND THERE WAS. AND IT WAS GOOD. AMEN.

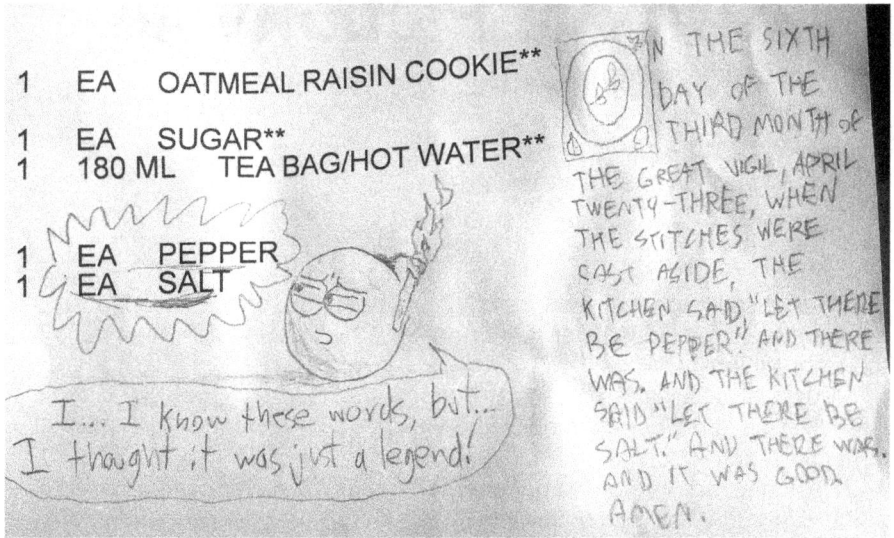

After over 2 months, someone from the kitchen mentions, "You know, as long as you don't have a medical condition against it you can request salt and pepper packets to be included with meals."

AYFKM, NOW you mention this? They're tiny packets, about a quarter the size of the sugar packet, but they can really save many of these meals.

Remember I mentioned about humidity making the paper sugar packets sometimes awkward to open efficiently? Make that four times more of a pain with these lil suckers. Often I rip the whole packet in half, through the slightly congealed contents, (sometimes resulting in a congealed clump falling in one spot) to dump half in the lil cup o soup, and the other half to sprinkle randomly across the food on the plate, like pixie dust, in hopes it would fly!

At this point, over 2 months... OH, add the nearly 2 months of my stay 2 years ago, we're looking at 4 months of salt-less eating. That sound ok? Sure, at home, we don't use a salt shaker at all.. but the home food naturally has salt content! Hospital food somehow dodges the naturally occurring instances of salt.

City of Fictionville
City Works and Sanitation

May 7th, 2017
Re: Hazardous recreational activity.

Dear residents,

Well, it seems that protein disposal has been reasonably stopped from both compost and sewer lines. Unfortunately, the damage has been done to the local ecology.

Muscular flies lead to muscular frogs, and so on.

As of this time, our river looks like a giant game of frogger, with muscular frogs, flies, and gators.

Residents are advised to not attempt to cross the river by jumping from gator to gator. At the time of this writing, two have already died, and I don't think we can afford another life.

To attempt to counter the unruly wildlife situation, I have volunteered myself for training and equipment in a program called Protective Animal Containment.

Thank you,
Hugh Sorte,
Director of Sanitation,
PAC man in training

PS: Rumours of the river now being haunted by ghosts is entirely tasteless and disrespectful to those who have lost their lives trying to play frogger. Why the colourful rumour always mentions four ghosts, when only two have died is a little confusing.

PPS: Whoever sent me the yellow raincoat, thank you.

So, I was cleared for limited time back in my wheelchair. Two years ago when I was allowed back in my chair, my arm muscles had weakened, and it felt like I was riding on flat tires. It was just mild atrophy.

This time, I had been lifting weights in bed to prevent such a thing. I got into my chair, and it... had flat tires. Not mega flat, but enough that it felt sluggish. But this would not stop my quest to go get junk food from the gift shop or the cafeteria.

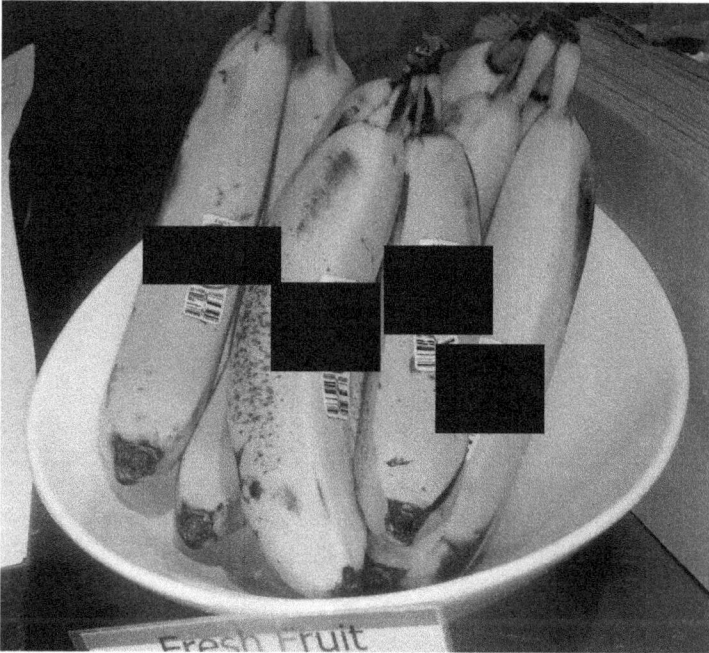

In the cafeteria, by the till, I saw this bowl of bananas.

Did these fruit (identities concealed for their protection) realize that their lost brethren had been taken away to be turned into cake, or simply cut in half? Did any whole banana ever make it back from a tray to report?

This group's human overlord was nearby at the till, so I couldn't speak freely with them, to tell them the fate of the missing, and at least bring them closure. #sad.

While I stared guiltily at the bananas, an ally loomed behind me. A small counter with things like ketchup, to pump into little containers for whatever meal a person might have gotten at the cafeteria, packets of salt and pepper, things like that... And a big kitchen-grade container of chili flakes.

Spice! I had found the spice! I claimed a little container, and half filled it, not want to look *too* greedy.. I knew where it was now, and could come back another day when my supply ran low...

Also nearby was a picnic-style squeeze bottle labeled in sharpie "FRANK'S RED HOT". *THAT* was a trap. Yes, Frank's has a level of heat I like, and a sauce is more functional physically on more types of food than flakes are, but unfortunately, the underlying flavour of Frank's... uh...

Look, I don't wanna get sued here, I've met people who love Frank's. It's a hugely successful brand. It indeed brings a respectable level of heat.

By the way, I always found the Frank's ad campaign funny where the catch phrase was "I put that shit on everything.".

Indeed it is.

I happily took my chili flakes, and left.

1   EA *spicy* CRANBERRY JUICE**

2   EA *spicy* CHICKEN THIGH & GRAVY**

1   120 ML *spicy* MASHED POTATO**
1   120 ML *spicy* PEAS & CORN**

1   125 ML *spicy* MANDARIN ORANGES**

1   EA *spicy* SUGAR**
1   180 ML *spicy* TEA BAG/HOT WATER**

1   EA *spicy* PEPPER
1   EA *spicy* SALT

GUESS WHO FOUND THE CHILI FLAKES DOWN IN THE CAFETERIA AND ISNT AFRAID TO USE EM?

Okay, only the chicken, the mash, and the vegggies got the flakes. Flakes don't stick that well to plain peas and corn. Shoulda mixed the peas and corn in with the mash. For that matter, for all the flakes tried with the chicken, they couldn't make it less fatty.

Mash was the main winner this day. Chili flakes, salt, pepper... nearly 3 months here, and I was just getting a system for all of this. (grumble grumble, could have had salt and pepper all along....)

A volunteer in school aiming to eventually be a doctor gave me a speech about salt. Yeah. Yeah, I know, but he isn't eating this stuff. Normal food has salt in it without additives. I don't even mean normal food you think of as being salty. The hospital takes normal foods and somehow removes naturally occurring salt. Voodoo, I suspect. Or alien interference. Adding a bit of salt after the fact is only returning balance to nature.

120 ML *SPICY* LACTAID MILK**
EA *SPICY* ORANGE JUICE**
ORAL 237 ML *SPICY* RESOURCE 2.0

180 ML *SPICY* CHEERIOS**

EA *SPICY* PEANUT BUTTER**

EA *SPICY* BISCUIT**
EA *SPICY* GRAPE JELLY**
EA *SPICY* MARGARINE**

EA *SPICY* SUGAR**
180 ML *SPICY* TEA BAG/HOT WATER

CHILI FLAKES, CHILI FLAKES, CHILI FLAKES, CHILI FLAKES!

THOUGH HONESTLY, CHILI FLAKES ARE NOT THAT SPICY.

TOMORROW, WE QUEST FOR SRIRACHA!

R. R   BREAKFAST

I think you can buy spicy peanut butter out there. I have a hunch.

I *know* you can get bacon-anything. I like bacon well enough, but I joke about it being so amazing... it's the stereotypical manfood. You can get bacon flavored gum, bacon scented deodorant, you name it.

Know where you *can't* get bacon?

Here.

Eh, and mosques, Hebrew temples, libraries. What's with that? Libraries, pick up your game already!

Medical supplies. Blood for my infusions ever since the surgery.

.....not buyin' it? Yeah, okay, fine. Soy sauce. I saw them on the same outing as when I got my chili flakes, but didn't grab any then. I don't know why not. I picked these up on another trip.

I was thinking of using them for mashed potatoes next time they happen to cross my tray. Only after did I think of using them on something like rice. Soy sauce on rice? Has anyone ever tried that? Crazy idea, huh?

Thankfully, they don't say anything about being sodium-free or anything like that. I fell in love with soy sauce *because* of the sodium.

Maybe I should have grabbed a few more...

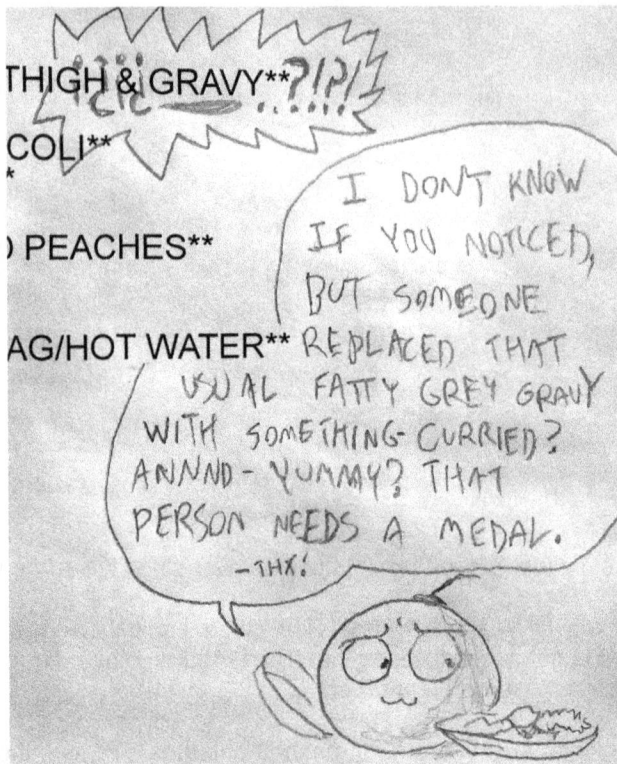

THIGH & GRAVY**?!?!?

COLI**
*

) PEACHES**

AG/HOT WATER**

I DON'T KNOW IF YOU NOTICED, BUT SOMEONE REPLACED THAT USUAL FATTY GREY GRAVY WITH SOMETHING CURRIED? ANNND- YUMMY? THAT PERSON NEEDS A MEDAL.
-THX!

"Chicken Thigh & Gravy" has become my enemy. I don't know if it's gotten worse in the last few months, or if I've gotten pickier. I spend 5-10 minutes trying to identify the remove fatty edges on the chicken, which is hard when it's doing the backstroke in greasy, khaki gravy. The gravy also does its best to permeate anything else on the plate. Is that little white bit a floating bit of mash, or an errant bit of fat? And this is a really frequently occurring dish. Often, it'll attack at lunch one day, then re-appear for dinner the day after, like they're hunting in pairs.

This day, I didn't have a huge appetite to begin with , wasn't feeling so hot, a tad grumpy, and dinner lands. The paper slip is sticking out to me. I yank it, and what do I see listed? CHICKEN THIGH & GRAVY.

I hadn't opened the cover yet, but it was staring at me. I felt a little exasperated with it. I slipped onto facebook on my phone for a sec just to post in all caps "CHICKEN THIGH & GRAVY" They'd understand. I've complained about it before on FB. And a handful of pages back, I think.

I rallied my tolerance, and lifted the lid, ready to begin operation. LO! NO GREASY FATTY GRAVY! Some kind of reddish curry sauce. HUZZAH!

The chicken under the sauce was still the same fatty stuff, but it was easier to operate, and the fact that someone downstairs changed it for me, (maybe not-so-officially, as the paper slip was the same as usual) was greatly appreciated.

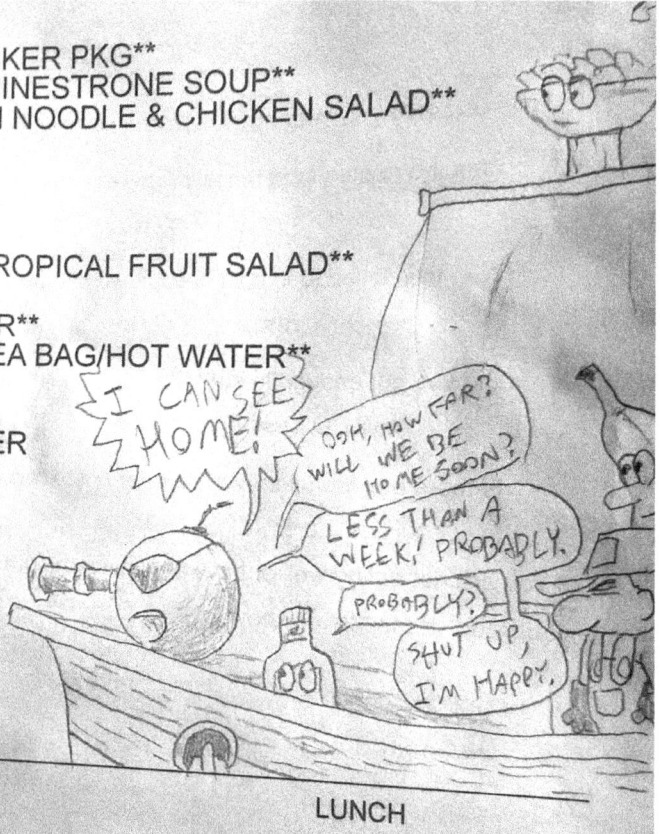

```
1   EA    CRACKER PKG**
1   180 ML    MINESTRONE SOUP**
2   EA    ASIAN NOODLE & CHICKEN SALAD**


1   125 ML    TROPICAL FRUIT SALAD**

1   EA   SUGAR**
    180 ML    TEA BAG/HOT WATER**

    EA   PEPPER
    EA   SALT
```

ACTR, R

LUNCH

With the number of blockades dwindling, we were able to set a tentative date for my return home. May 17th, exactly three months after I checked in. As I write this, (I've been working on the book for most of my stay) it is May 12th.

When I get home, I'll be in a hospital bed again, and still fairly limited for how much time I can be 'up' in my wheelchair, but I'll be home. More time with the wife & kids beyond weekend visits. Access to TV, or more importantly 3 months of PVR recordings of the few shows I watch. Playstation. Wifi. Broadband internet. My pets! A lack of random hospital beeping!

Oh, and non-hospital food! Okay, there's been some diamonds in the rough here.. well, zirconiums, at least, but on the whole.. Hey, remember pasta? I remember pasta. How about chicken that isn't lined with fat and swimming in... fat.

Again, my thanks and gratitude to the nurses, doctors, wound specialists, OT, and of course the kitchen crew who go to heroic efforts to do the most good with what they're given to deal with.

May this be my last hospital food encounter for a long, long time.!

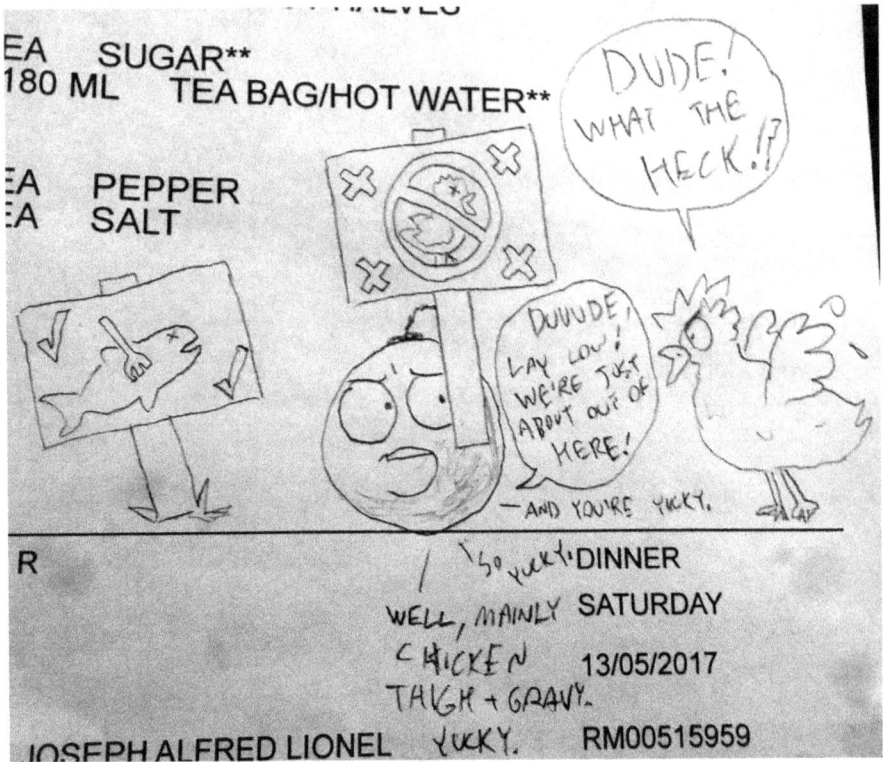

EA SUGAR**
180 ML TEA BAG/HOT WATER**

EA PEPPER
EA SALT

DUDE! WHAT THE HECK.!?

DUUUDE! LAY LOW! WE'RE JUST ABOUT OUT OF HERE!

— AND YOU'RE YUCKY.

R

'SO YUCKY' DINNER
WELL, MAINLY SATURDAY
CHICKEN 13/05/2017
THIGH + GRAVY.
JOSEPH ALFRED LIONEL YUCKY. RM00515959

One last official protest to the kitchen on how bad 'CHICKEN THIGH & GRAVY' is. I'm just tempting fate now. Two days and I'm outta here.*

In this doodle, we ask again- do these foods realize what their destiny is? Why is a grape the same size as a chicken? Am I implying I want to take a like chicken home with me?

I don't, for the record. I've had chickens. I hate eggs. I hate dodging chicken poop landmines to escape my yard. I liked the chicken personally though.

*at the time of writing that, I didn't know there'd be 2 more days delay. #notsofastpunk

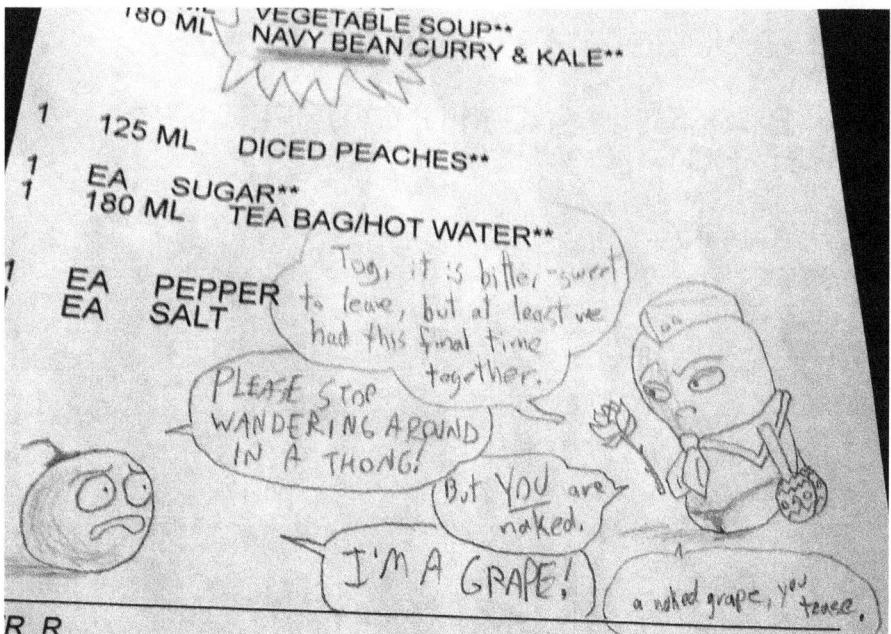

Navy Bean, Spicy to the last.

I was hoping I'd run into this dish again before I went, party because it's yummy, has a touch of zest, and of course because Navy Bean is a fun character.

I thought I was going home today, (as I write this, it is the exact three month mark of my checking into the hospital on this stay), but an equipment delay for home meant two more days here. Without these extra days, I wouldn't have run into Navy Bean again.

Of course, there are down sides. I'm not home for my son's birthday tomorrow, (he doesn't seem to care, he's just excited I'm coming home soon,) and I'm in the hospital for that smidgen longer. I did a little math, and between this stay, the last stay two years ago, and my six months right after my accident, that's been about a year of me in hospitals. Nearly 2.5% of my life. There are those who have it far worse, but it was just an odd way to think of time, like the moment to realize you slept away a third of your life.

Hey, let's do a little more math... on this trip alone, let's just call it 90 days.. times 3 meals...270. And my stay 2 years ago? 147 meals. GF Strong after my accident? About 540 meals. That's 957 meals. Dang. Another 15 days of meals, and I'd have had over 1000. (Way to jinx myself, huh?)

At this time, I expect I'll be having three or four more meals in here. One or two of them are breakfasts. The other two are a chance for my arch rival to attack... CHICKEN THIGH & GRAVY... Stay tuned...

COD NUGGET & TARTAR SAUCE**

ML   BROCCOLI AND MINI CAULIFLOWER**
RED POTATO WEDGES**

BANANA

SUGAR**
ML   TEA BAG/HOT WATER**

WE MADE IT OUT WITHOUT RUNNING INTO CHICKEN THIGH & GRAVY AGAIN! JUST ONE MORE BREAKFAST, AND I'M OUTTA HERE!

PEPPER
SALT

THEY MOSTLY COME OUT AT NIGHT.

MOSTLY.

DINNER

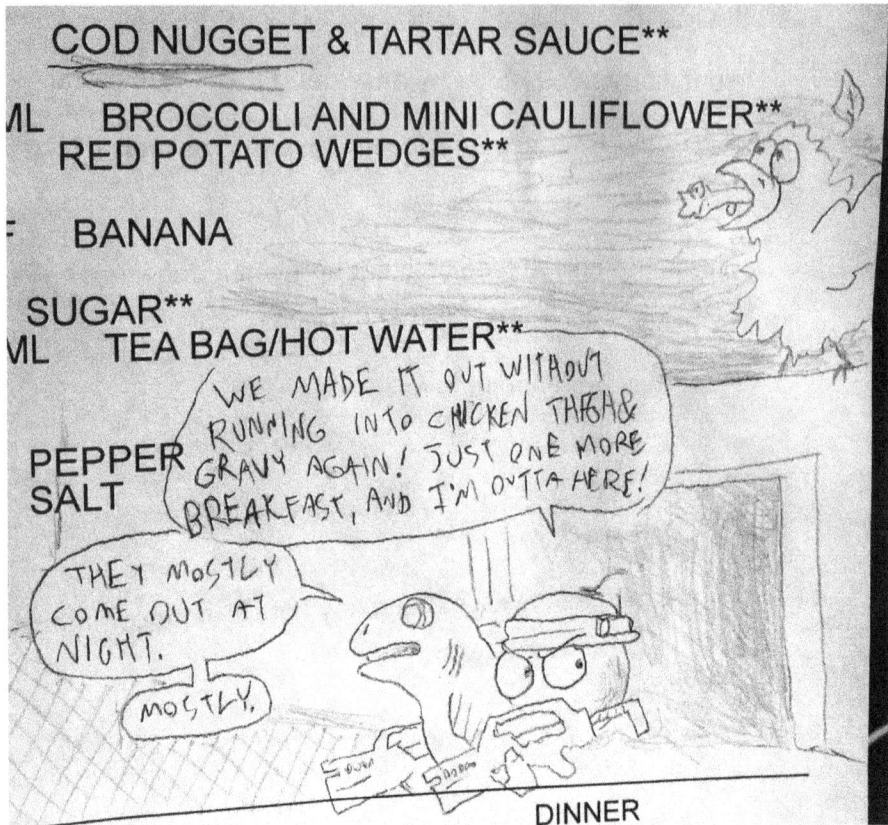

I was considering spoofing the last supper painting for my last supper, but... I had myself convinced I'd be getting 'chicken thigh & gravy'...

I heard a nurse telling some patient somewhere down the hall that supper was coming, and I found myself gripped with dread.

It was coming for me.

I heard the rattle of the cart that carries the stack of trays carrying people's meals. What direction was that? How far? 15 meters? 10 meters?

I heard the squeak that the trays make when pulled from the clamps that secure it in the cart... 5 meters?

I remembered a scene where space marines were tracking an incoming horde of aliens... ever closer, bit by bit. I heard the cart moving again, closer! I hear it! It rolled into sight! OH NOES! HERE COMES THE TRAY! BRING IT, CHCKEN! I ALWAYS KNEW IT WAS GOING TO END LIKE THIS! GET OVER HERE, I'LL CUT YOU!!!

Oh. Fish. I almost wish it was the chicken. For closure. Revenge.

I'm clear. I'm safe. No more meals where it can come get me. One more brekkie, and I'm out...!

Thanks to the kitchen staff for not poisoning me, and putting up with me,
Thanks to the doctors for poisoning me carefully so that I wouldn't be awake while they stabbed me for my own good.
Thanks to the nurses for ..... also not poisoning me, and putting up with me, and doing all they could to get me better, and their incredible patience with not only me, but the patients who often push them beyond reasonable expectations.

Really, only two of these people intentionally poisoned me, and only two stabbed me, and I approved those actions.

After both stabbings, I woke up wearing green socks that looked like they were stolen from Santa's elves.

I'm still not sure how I feel about that.

And of course thanks to you, the reader, for not poisoning me, and putting up with me.

Please take the time to check out my novels.

RUBBERMAN'S CAGE

Lenth grew up in a lie.

Apparently there's more than five people in the world.
Savage Citizens, orderly Providers, keepers of ignorance, and a damaged killer stand in the way of the world's simple truths.

Four Brothers live their lives in an enclosed habitat as directed by the silent Rubberman above them. When they disobey, they get shocked. This is normal. It always has been.
When a Brother dies, they learn of death. When he is replaced by someone new, they learn they are replaceable.
When the ceiling above the ceiling cracks open, Lenth plans a journey beyond the known universe:
A third floor.

Up.

Coming soon, the second book in the Rubberman series:

RUBBERMAN'S
CITIZENS

In Citizenry, Leena knew cruelty was normal.

Order was kept by Warren, through intimidation and abuse.
Normal meant hearing screams, and knowing no one dared help.

Normal was knowing that tomorrow,
it could be your own screams being ignored.

Leena found a way to help. Leena found a chance.
Leena discovered revolution.

Also check out the Lifehack series!

Independent of the Rubberman series, the Lifehack series concludes in book three, although all are complete stories unto themselves.

They all deal with the same fictional nation, and the dangers of nanotechnology in the wrong hands. A few minor characters appear in multiple books, and some themes are shared.

They're been occasionally called 'hard' science fiction, because they don't involve the typical space-opera tropes. No space travel, no aliens, no phasers. Science is not used like magic, and the tech is very 'near future'.

Unlike much hard science-fiction, the books don't spend a lot of time explaining the little technical details beyond what drives the story. They are largely character-driven.

While Lifehack and Echoes of Erebus have some heavy action, and a pile of reanimated monsters, Watching Yute (book #2) sets a different pace, where the nanotechnology subject is very much present, the focus in Watching Yute ultimately is on loss and mourning. I feel the need to warn people that Yute doesn't have a happy ending. Thus has caused some people to skip Watching Yute... and some people so start with it.

It wants the reader to suffer. It makes me suffer, and I love it for that. That aside, a sense of humour manages to sneak in now and then.

LIFEHACK

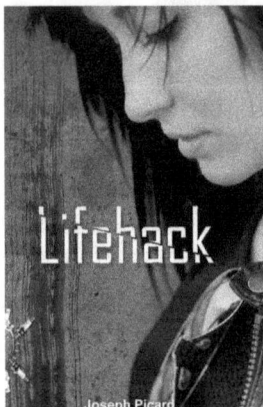

Regan has her ups and downs.
- Dumping her girlfriend: Down.
- Moving in with her loving brother: Up.
- Waking up to a plague of undead: REALLY down.

After the undead began roaming the neighborhood, Regan lost track of her brother. She's spent the last two years searching for him. In the meantime, she's fallen in love, only to be told, "Sorry, I'm straight. And you're a lunatic." There's a psycho out there somewhere who caused the outbreak, using nanotechnology, just for the fun of it, and Regan intends to hunt him down.

Oh, and the crush she still has on the straight gal? Dangerously distracting, when there's a zombie around every corner.
http://www.amazon.com/Lifehack-Joseph-Picard-ebook/dp/B0088LI9CY/

WATCHING YUTE

An ideal post opened up for Lieutenant Cassidy Stanton when she wanted a fresh start. She expected a measure of peace, guarding a historic temple in the middle of the desert.

She didn't expect to find a new girlfriend; maybe even a soul mate.
She didn't expect to be in the crossfire of a terrorist, a cowardly scientist, and a fleet of microscopic invaders.

She didn't expect to lose.

http://www.amazon.com/Watching-Yute-Lifehack-Book-2-ebook/dp/B008A7SRJG/

ECHOES OF EREBUS

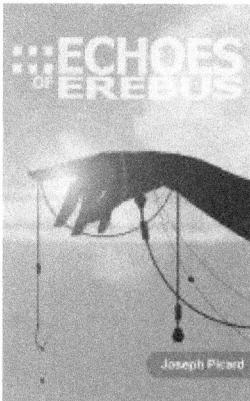

Sarah's got daddy issues. He lives in her head, built her out of fish, and killed millions of people. But he's really sorry.
Honest.

A father that lives in your head wouldn't be so bad if he wasn't the killer of millions. At least it's comforting to know that he didn't murder the fishes used to create your body.
Or the seagull. Sarah hides her illegal nanite origins in an effort to build an ordinary life, but the legacy of dad's horrors makes it difficult. Especially when new, but familiar zombie-like abominations begin to appear in the city.

http://www.amazon.com/Echoes-Erebus-Lifehack-Book-3-ebook/dp/B008AFPH6O/

Find Joseph Picard's books at:
OZERO.CA

Amazon.com http://www.amazon.com/Joseph-Picard/e/B002LPT7VA/

www.ingramcontent.com/pod-product-compliance
Lightning Source LLC
Chambersburg PA
CBHW031556040426
42452CB00006B/320